E.C.

*Please Don't Take
Mummy Away*

Also by Maggie Hartley

Please Don't Take Mummy Away

THE TRUE STORY OF SISTERS LEFT FRIGHTENED, COLD AND ALONE

MAGGIE HARTLEY

WITH
HEATHER BISHOP

SEVEN DIALS

First published in Great Britain in 2024 by Seven Dials,
an imprint of The Orion Publishing Group Ltd
Carmelite House, 50 Victoria Embankment
London EC4Y 0DZ

An Hachette UK Company

1 3 5 7 9 10 8 6 4 2

A CIP catalogue record for this book is
available from the British Library.

ISBN (Mass Market Paperback) 978 1 3996 2088 8
ISBN (eBook) 978 1 3996 2089 5
ISBN (Audio) 978 1 3996 2090 1

Typeset by Born Group
Printed and bound in Great Britain by Clays Ltd, Elcograf S.p.A.

MIX
Paper from
responsible sources
FSC® C104740

www.orionbooks.co.uk

Dedication

This book is dedicated to Coco, Lola and Amena and all the children who have passed through my home. It's been a privilege to have cared for you and to be able to share your stories. And to the children who live with me now: thank you for your determination, strength and joy and for sharing your lives with me.

Contents

A Message from Maggie

I wanted to write this book to give people an honest account of what it's like to be a foster carer. To talk about some of the challenges that I face on a day-to-day basis and some of the children that I've helped.

My main concern throughout all this is to protect the children who have been in my care. For this reason, all names and identifying details have been changed, including my own, and no locations have been included.

Being a foster carer is a privilege and I couldn't imagine doing anything else. My house is never quiet but I wouldn't have it any other way. I hope perhaps my stories will inspire other people to consider fostering as new carers are always desperately needed. In fact, the latest statistics are alarming. Ofsted figures from 2022 showed that the number of available homes for foster children in England had fallen by almost a quarter in four years. This comes at the same time as the number of children in the UK care system is at a record high. Foster carers are needed more than ever so please do look into it if it's something that you or someone you know has ever considered.

Maggie Hartley

Prologue

The call came through on the radio of the police car just as they were taking the first bite of the sandwiches they'd bought at the supermarket. PC Caroline Davidson looked wearily at her shift partner, PC Robbie Hunt.

'Shoplifter at a corner shop,' he sighed. 'Hardly the crime of the century.'

Normally a shoplifter would be way down on their list of callouts but, for once in as long as Caroline could remember, it had been a quiet night shift so far.

'We'd better go,' she told him. 'It's only two minutes down the road.'

'Really?' he said and she nodded.

'OK then,' he sighed, turning the engine on. 'You can be the one who gives the teenager the lecture while they spit and swear at you.'

The shop, a little off-licence and mini-market, was a one-minute drive from where they were parked. To be honest, they probably could have walked there quicker.

The door of the shop beeped loudly as they pushed it open. There was a disgruntled-looking elderly man sitting behind the counter on a stool.

'About time,' he sighed. 'She's in the stockroom. This ain't the first time she's done it. She's in here every few days, thinks she can just take what she wants. I knew she was up to something, only this time the shop was quiet so I spotted her on the cameras. It'll be on CCTV so there's proof. I want her done for this.'

Her, thought Caroline.

For some reason, she'd assumed it would be a teenaged boy.

'Probably a druggie,' the shopkeeper sighed. 'She's got that look about her. Skinny as a rake with weird eyes that stare right through you.'

He turned the sign to 'Closed', locked the shop door and led them through to the back.

'Here she is,' he told them.

Cowering in the corner of the stockroom was a young woman. Caroline had been expecting a teenager and although she was young, the lines etched on the woman's face suggested that she was older.

She looked up at them with fearful green eyes.

'I told you I'd call the police on you,' the shopkeeper raged. 'You've been stealing from me for months, making a mockery of my livelihood. Well you're gonna pay for it big time now.'

The woman was silent but Caroline could see that she was shaking with fear.

'Go on then,' he hissed. 'What you got to say for yourself?'

'I'm sorry,' she said in a voice so quiet, it was almost a whisper.

'She's admitting it,' the shopkeeper nodded triumphantly.

2

'Please just let me go,' begged the young woman. 'I promise I won't do it again. I'll pay you back for it all. Just tell me how much I owe you and I'll find a way.'

The shopkeeper laughed then he turned to Caroline and Robbie.

'I want to press charges,' he said. 'I've got the CCTV footage I can give you.'

'OK,' said Robbie. 'Let's get you down to the station.'

The woman gasped and put her head in her hands.

'Please,' she said. 'I'm begging you. Don't make me come down to the station. I can come another time but not now.'

'I'm afraid you can't pick and choose when we interview you,' Robbie told her. 'We'll need to take you down to the station to get a few details and ask you some questions.'

The woman was in floods of tears.

'Please don't do this,' she sobbed. 'I'm begging you.'

There was something about this frail young woman that made Caroline think they were being overzealous.

'Can I have a quick word?' she asked her colleague.

She and Robbie stepped outside the stockroom.

'Do we really have to make an example out of her like this?' she said in a low voice. 'It's just shoplifting. She looks desperate.'

'You heard the man,' he told her. 'He's got CCTV proof that she's broken the law. We can't just ignore it. Besides, if we take her to the station and give her a scare, it might stop her doing it again. Might give her another way to support her habit.'

Yes, she was thin and her face was so hollow you could see her cheekbones, but there was something about the young woman's appearance that told Caroline she wasn't on drugs.

3

'I just think she's been taught enough of a lesson,' she shrugged.

But there was no talking her colleague round.

The shopkeeper came out to join them.

'Are you gonna cuff her then?' he nodded. 'Send out a message to other scumbags who think it's OK to rip me off on a daily basis?'

'I don't think there's any need for that,' Robbie told him.

'Just one quick question,' Caroline asked him. 'What did she steal?'

He walked over to the till.

'This lot,' he said, putting an array of items on the counter. 'I reckon I caught her before she could get to the booze.'

Caroline looked at the items on the counter – a loaf of white bread, a carton of milk, some jam and crisps. But it was the final items that concerned her the most – two bottles of Calpol and a packet of pull-ups in a toddler size. Her heart sank.

'Let me have another word with her,' she said.

She went back into the stockroom where the young woman was sitting on a stool crying. Caroline perched down next to her.

'What's your name, darling?' she asked her.

'Zoe,' she whimpered.

'I saw the pull-ups that you stole, Zoe,' she told her. 'Do you have a child at home? Is that why you don't want to go down to the station with us?'

The woman didn't say a word, she just buried her head in her hands and sobbed.

'Please don't make me go to the station,' she said. 'I'm begging you. I need to go home.'

'Is your child home alone?' Caroline asked.

The woman sobbed even louder.

'Just let me go home. I promise I'll come to the station tomorrow.'

She looked up at her with desperate eyes.

Robbie came back in.

'Right then,' he said. 'Let's go.'

'Please don't do this,' sobbed the woman.

Caroline pulled her colleague to one side.

'Before we go anywhere, I think we need to call Social Services,' she said. 'It's an emergency.'

ONE

A Waiting Game

Looking across the table at Graham, I chinked my glass with his.

'Cheers,' I said, before I took a sip of my white wine. 'It's great to see you again.'

'It's been a while, hasn't it?' he smiled, his blue eyes twinkling.

Graham and I had known each other for years and we'd dated in the past. But we had gradually come to the realisation that we were both so busy that neither of us could commit to anything serious. We still cared about each other though and we liked to meet up from time to time for a walk or, like tonight, a meal out, but lately that's as far as it went. My fostering meant that I rarely had the time or indeed the energy for a night out. Graham had his own commitments too. He was a physiotherapist and during the week he mostly worked away at his friend's practice on the other side of the country. He also had family abroad so he liked to use his holidays to go and visit them. It had been months since we'd managed to meet up but it was lovely to finally spend some time together again.

'So,' he asked, taking a sip of his red wine. 'Are things as busy as usual?'

'Yep,' I smiled.

It always was when it came to fostering. Sadly, the number of children being taken into care was only increasing while the number of foster carers was declining so there were never enough homes for them to go to.

'Who have you got with you at the moment?' he asked. 'Although I know you're probably not allowed to say much.'

Graham had known me long enough to understand that for confidentiality and child protection reasons, I would never disclose any personal information about a child or why they'd been taken into care.

'Well, you've actually caught me at a quietish time,' I explained. 'I've just had a sibling group of four kids leave.'

'Four?' he gasped. 'No wonder I've not heard much from you in a while.'

'Yep, three girls and a boy,' I replied. 'It has been pretty full-on, to be honest.'

Riley, five, and his sisters Lula, six, Katie, seven, and nine-year-old Maddie, had been with me for the past six months. Their mother, Carlie, was a single parent who had been preyed on by a series of abusive men who had seemingly just used her and her flat as a place to take or deal drugs. All of the children had different fathers and slowly, with drugs all around her, Carlie had eventually been sucked into that lifestyle too. When the children had been taken into care, Carlie had just found out she was pregnant with twins who, more than likely, would be taken away from her at birth.

In the past year, as Carlie's drug addiction had worsened, the children had largely been left to look after themselves. By the time they'd come to me, they were dirty, hungry and traumatised. It had been a hard few months but consistency, boundaries and a routine had given them safety and security, and gradually they'd started to trust me and their behaviour had improved.

Eventually, Carlie's mother and sister, both of whom she'd been estranged from for years, had taken on the four children between them under an arrangement that was known as Kinship Care, where relatives or other adults who have a close connection to a child agree to care for them. They lived hundreds of miles away at the other end of the country but it was the fresh start the children needed. Sadly, Carlie had stopped coming to contact sessions to see them and had refused to cooperate with Social Services any more. In fact, at this point in time, they didn't even know where she was.

Children this age were never going to be healed overnight but with family around to love and support them, hopefully the four of them could start to work through it.

Even though it had been an intense few months, the house seemed so empty and quiet without the four of them tearing around. Riley had been wild when he had first come to me but slowly, a loving little boy had emerged and the girls really looked after their little brother.

'I don't miss the noise and the constant mess but I miss their little faces,' I told Graham wistfully. 'But I've already got a new placement.'

As usual there had been no time to mope. Literally hours after they had left, I'd got a call from my agency asking if I could take on another child. Amena was fifteen and a refugee from Somalia. She and her mother, Hodan, had been in the UK for several years but her aunt had suddenly become seriously ill in France and Hodan had gone to look after her. Amena had been with me for a couple of weeks and she was a sweet girl. Even though she was a teenager, I didn't feel comfortable leaving her on her own in the house at night because she hadn't been with me that long. Babysitters had to be over twenty-one and police-checked, so I'd asked my long-term foster daughter Louisa to come round and sit with her.

'I've left her with Louisa,' I told him. 'So I can't be late back, I'm afraid, as she's got work in the morning.'

'How is Louisa?' asked Graham.

'She's great,' I nodded. 'Can you believe Edie is two already?'

I'd taken Louisa in as a teenager after both her parents had died in a car accident. She was all grown up now – she worked as a nanny, was married to Charlie and they had a daughter called Edie. Although I'd never formally adopted Louisa, she was for all intents and purposes like my biological daughter and Edie called me 'Nana'.

'She's the sweetest little thing,' I smiled. 'She's talking now and she's so funny. She likes bossing me around as she knows she's got me wrapped around her little finger.'

'Have you got any photos?' he asked.

'Are you joking?' I laughed. 'I've got a phone full of them.'

I'd just got my mobile out of my bag to show Graham a picture of Edie when it started buzzing in my hand.

'Oh,' I laughed. 'That made me jump.'

I glanced at the number on the screen.

'It's my fostering agency. I'm so sorry, I'd better answer this.'

Graham nodded. We'd been in this situation all too frequently before when our dates had been cut short by a call from Social Services or my agency.

I'd been with my agency for years and I pretty much knew all of the staff there. One of the duty workers, Janet, was calling.

'Hi Maggie,' she said. 'I'm sorry to disturb your evening but Social Services have just been in touch. They're urgently looking for a placement for two young children who've just been taken into care tonight.'

Not all agencies took on emergency placements but mine was one of the few in my area that did. Janet didn't have many details at this stage but I listened as she explained more.

'I'm afraid I've only got the briefest of details but sadly it looks like a neglect case,' she said. 'Police arrested the mum and it turns out that she had two kids who had been left home alone.

'It's two little girls,' she added. 'I'm afraid I don't have their names or ages but the social worker will be able to tell you more.'

Social Services needed somewhere for them to go tonight while they assessed the situation and the police interviewed their mother.

It was nearly 9 p.m., and the thought of two little ones not having anywhere to go on a dark, freezing February night made me feel sick. I had two designated bedrooms for my fostering – Amena was in the smaller one, which meant I had a larger room with bunk beds and a single bed sitting there empty. I knew I couldn't say no.

'Poor little things,' I sighed. 'I'd be happy to help. Where are they now?'

Janet explained that they were currently with the out-of-hours social worker – a woman named Arti – at their mother's flat. The children were being taken into care under an Emergency Protection Order, known as an EPO. This was reserved for children who Social Services felt were most at risk and needed to come into the care system as soon as possible. Judges were available 24/7 to issue EPOs but it could take anything from an hour or more for the paperwork to come through.

'I'll ring Arti back and tell her that as soon as the EPO comes through, to bring them straight to you,' Janet added.

'OK,' I replied. 'I'm out at the moment but I'll get home as soon as I can.'

As I hung up and put my phone down on the table, I could see the disappointment in Graham's eyes.

'I'm sorry,' I sighed. 'An emergency placement has come in – two little ones who've just been taken into care.'

'It's OK,' he replied. 'I know it's part and parcel of the job. Let's catch up another time.'

I nodded, but I think we both knew that that probably wasn't likely to be anytime soon. I gave him a quick hug and a kiss on the cheek and grabbed my handbag.

As I rushed out of the pub to my car, I felt incredibly guilty. This was why it was so difficult as a single foster carer to ever meet anyone or hold down a serious relationship.

But as I drove the twenty-minute journey home, all I could think about were those two little girls. I didn't know their names or ages yet, but I could imagine their fear at being taken away late at night by strangers.

I went through the usual checklists in my head. Thankfully I always had the bedrooms made up with clean bedding for situations like tonight. All those years ago in my early twenties when I'd started fostering, I'd learnt that children came into care suddenly and at all times of the day and night. Being as prepared as possible really helped to save time. I had a huge cupboard of essentials, such as clean towels, toothbrushes and flannels. I also had underwear, socks and pyjamas and a few basic clothes in as many sizes as I could store. I tended to grab stuff from the supermarket or the shops when there was a sale on. I didn't know these girls' ages yet but I was sure I would have something that would tide them over until the following day when I could get to the shops. I also had nappies and a few baby essentials in the loft but I hadn't got the impression from the duty worker that these girls were babies.

Finally, I was home.

I walked through the front door to find Louisa watching TV in the front room.

'Oh, you're back early,' she said. 'You must have eaten quickly.'

'I didn't even have time for dinner sadly,' I told her.

I explained about the call from Social Services and that two children were on their way to me that night. Louisa had grown up around my fostering throughout her teenage years so she was used to kids coming and going at all times of the day.

'Poor things,' she sighed. 'They must be so scared.'

She'd always been empathetic to what other children were going through in a strange new environment as she'd been through it herself all those years ago. But having Edie had given her a deeper understanding of how terrified little ones must feel.

'I can stay a while, so is there anything I can do to help you get sorted?' she asked.

'That's really kind of you, lovey, but there isn't really much I can do at this point,' I told her. 'You know me, the beds in the big bedroom are already made and I've got PJs and toothbrushes in the cupboard. I've got enough stuff that we can make do tonight.'

I wasn't sure if the girls would be coming with any belongings. Sadly, when it came to neglect, most children arrived with either nothing or a black bin bag of tatty, dirty clothes.

'I'll leave you to it then,' said Louisa. 'Let me know if there's anything I can do. I can always nip out to the big supermarket for you.'

'Thanks, flower,' I smiled. 'That's sweet of you. I'll drop you a text tomorrow.'

She explained Amena was upstairs reading.

'She's been no bother,' she told me. 'She's such a sweet girl.'

'I'd better go and tell her what's going on,' I said.

I stood on the doorstep and waved Louisa off. As I was closing the front door, my phone beeped with a text.

Hope it all goes OK. It was lovely to see you (briefly!). Graham x

I still felt guilty for leaving so abruptly when we hadn't seen each other for ages.

Sorry, I replied. *Let's try and meet up again another time x.*

Now I had to focus on the girls who would soon be arriving on my doorstep.

I went upstairs to see Amena who was on her bed listening to music.

'How are you doing?' I asked her.

'Good,' she said. 'Me and Louisa watched some TV then I came up here. I got a phone call from my mum too.'

'Oh that's good,' I replied. 'How's your aunt doing?'

'Not great,' she said sadly. 'But I know she's glad to have Mum there.'

I told her about the girls.

'I'm expecting them to arrive anytime soon,' I told her.

'Oh no, that's really sad,' she sighed. 'I bet they're really scared.'

'It's very late for little ones,' I nodded.

I imagined that they'd be so exhausted they'd just want to sleep, but I wasn't sure what kind of a state they would be in.

When children suddenly came into the care system because of neglect, they often arrived in the most awful conditions. I'd experienced all sorts of distressing things from children whose hair was crawling with so many lice you could see it moving, to skin that was red-raw and covered in sores because they'd been left to sit in their own excrement.

Even though it was late, there was the possibility they would need a bath. I also dug out some nit shampoo, just in case, as it was always a good temporary measure before I had a chance to get out the lotion and nit comb the following day.

I made myself a sandwich and a cup of tea, all the while listening for the sound of a car pulling up outside.

But by 10.30 p.m. there was still no news.

'Bed time, lovey,' I told Amena.

'When are the new children coming?' she asked me.

'I don't honestly know,' I shrugged. 'I'd hoped they'd be here by now but you've got school tomorrow and you can see them in the morning.'

'OK,' she nodded.

With Amena in bed, I got myself another cup of tea and went into the front room. I was as ready as I'd ever be and there was nothing more that I could do now.

I curled up on the sofa and sat there in the cosy glow of the lamp. I thought of putting the TV on but I knew I wouldn't be able to focus on anything.

Something told me that I was in for a long night. All I could do now was sit and wait for that knock on the door.

TWO

Clean and Tidy

That knock on the door finally came at 11.30 p.m.

'Coming,' I called, jumping up off the sofa.

As I walked out into the hallway, I could feel the adrenalin pumping through my body. I took a deep breath and tried to mentally prepare myself for what I was about to face. I'd fostered many neglected children over the years but it was something that you could never not be affected by. I didn't think I could ever become hardened to the horrors that some children had been put through by the very people who were supposed to love and protect them. Some of the things I'd seen were just utterly heartbreaking but I always made sure that I kept my emotions in check in front of the kids themselves.

I opened the door to see a petite woman who looked to be in her forties standing there in the darkness. She was wrapped up in a coat with a furry hood and a woolly hat.

'Hi Maggie,' she said in a soft voice, showing me her ID. 'I'm Arti, the duty social worker.'

I could see her warm breath in the cold air and the pavement was already twinkling with frost.

'Lovely to meet you,' I smiled but I was distracted by the two little girls standing either side of her. They both had wispy blonde hair and even though they each had a blanket wrapped around them, I could see they were shivering.

'Come on in,' I told them gently. 'It's freezing out there.'

As they shuffled into the hallway, I could finally see them properly in the light. The girls stared up at me suspiciously with scared green eyes.

'Maggie, this is Coco and Lola,' Arti told me. 'Coco is seven and Lola is three.'

'It's lovely to meet you,' I told them gently. 'It's very late and you must both be really tired.'

'I'm not tired,' said Lola defiantly.

'Where's our mummy?' asked Coco. 'Why did the police take her away?'

Arti and I exchanged looks.

'Remember we talked about this at the flat, Coco,' she reminded her gently. 'The police need Mummy to answer a few questions so while she's doing that, you're going to stay here with Maggie tonight.'

'Mummy come back soon?' asked Lola, looking confused.

'We'll know more in the morning, girls,' I told them gently. 'We need to get you to bed tonight, then hopefully Arti can talk to Mummy tomorrow.'

Bless them, I thought. I couldn't even begin to imagine what was going through their little heads right now.

'Let's all go through to the kitchen and I'll get you a beaker of warm milk each and a biscuit,' I told them.

As I heated the milk up in a pan, something struck me. I'd expected these girls to be dirty and unkempt. Admittedly, I couldn't see what they were wearing under the blankets but, on the face of it, they looked and smelt clean. Some children who arrived on my doorstep were so dirty that the second I opened the door, I could smell them. Coco and Lola were thin but their faces weren't gaunt and their eyes didn't have that blank, dull look that a lot of neglected and abused children had.

When the milk had warmed, I tipped it into two plastic beakers and put a couple of chocolate biscuits on a plate.

'Here you go, sweetie,' I said to Coco as I handed her the cup.

'Thank you,' she replied in a quiet voice.

Lola also said thank you as I handed her the milk and I was struck by their lovely manners.

'You have your milk, girls, while I have a quick chat with Arti,' I told them.

We stood in the kitchen area while they sat on the sofa over the other side of the room. When children have been taken into care, they behave in many different ways. If they've had no boundaries or routine at home then within a few seconds of being in my house they can be opening drawers, pulling out the contents of cupboards and jumping on the furniture. Some children are very fearful and quiet. Coco and Lola just sat there, quietly sipping their milk and looking around with a bewildered expression on their faces.

I put the kettle on and made Arti and I a cup of tea.

'Sorry it took us so long to get you,' she told me in a low voice. 'We were waiting for the paperwork to come through from the courts.'

'That's OK,' I replied. 'To be honest, I thought you'd be a lot later.'

I looked across at Coco and Lola, who were still sitting nicely on the sofa.

'What gorgeous girls,' I sighed. 'And they're both very well mannered. When Janet told me it was a neglect case, to be honest I was expecting the worst.'

'Well, as you and I know, Maggie, neglect can take many different forms and it definitely looks like neglect to me,' sighed Arti. 'They'd both been left home alone and, from what we can glean so far, I don't think it was a one-off.

'Mum is apparently a prolific shoplifter by all accounts,' she continued. 'The police threatened to take her down to the station and she panicked and eventually told them about the girls being left alone.'

'What was the flat like?' I asked her.

'It wasn't dirty as such but very bare,' sighed Arti. 'What little furniture there was, was old and threadbare. There were no proper beds – the girls were sleeping on the sofa cushions on the floor. They were frozen to the core. They had piles of blankets but there was no heating or even lights. The electricity bill had obviously not been paid for a while.

'There were a few candles around. They weren't lit but who knows what could have happened if the girls had got hold of some matches?'

Poor little mites, I thought. All alone in the dark on such a bitterly cold night.

Just then, Lola started to cough.

'Are you OK, sweetie?' I called over to her. 'Would you like a glass of water?'

She shook her head.

'She seems to have a bit of a nasty cough,' nodded Arti. 'So it's something to keep an eye on.'

'What happens now?' I asked her.

Arti explained that their mum, Zoe, had been taken to the police station.

'Child neglect is obviously a lot more serious an allegation than shoplifting so they've taken her in for questioning. I'm waiting to hear what's happened and if she's been charged with anything.'

'Is there a dad around?' I asked.

'I only had time for a brief chat with Mum before the police took her off and she was very upset,' she told me. 'But from what I can gather it's just her and the girls. A dad hasn't been mentioned.'

She'd checked Social Service's records and Mum wasn't previously known to them. Over the next few days, the EPO would give Social Services the chance to talk to Zoe, the police, Coco's teachers and anyone else involved with the family to try to start building up a picture of their home life.

'The girls will be assigned a social worker tomorrow so I imagine they'll get in touch with you in the morning.'

'OK,' I nodded.

'I'm afraid I'd better head back to the office now but you've got my number so please give me a call if you need anything else this evening,' she told me.

'Thanks so much,' I replied.

I knew all I could do tonight was to try and settle the girls as best as I could and hopefully they would be able to get some sleep.

'I'm assuming they didn't come with any belongings?' I asked Arti as she put her coat and hat back on.

'Oh, actually they did,' she said. 'Thanks for reminding me. Mum begged the police to let her quickly pack a few things for the girls so they've got a bag in the car. I'll go and get it.'

A minute later, Arti came back in.

'I've left it in the hallway,' she told me.

She turned to Coco and Lola.

'Bye-bye, girls,' she told them. 'I'm going to go now as it's very late and you need to try to get some sleep. But Maggie will look after you.'

They didn't say a word and they looked even more scared as they watched Arti leave.

'Don't worry, I can see myself out,' she told me.

It was nearly midnight by now and I wanted to start trying to get them settled.

'Right then,' I smiled. 'Let's go upstairs and I'll show you the bedroom where you'll both be sleeping as you must be very tired.'

'When's Mummy coming back?' Coco asked me.

'Remember what Arti said before?' I said gently. 'Mummy's talking to the police at the moment. You're going to sleep here at my house tonight but we'll know a bit more in the morning when we talk to your social worker.'

They still looked very confused.

'Your mummy packed you some things so let's bring them upstairs with us.'

'Mummy was sad,' sighed Lola. 'She was crying. The polices made her sad.'

'I'm sure Mummy's feeling better now and hopefully you can see her very soon,' I told them. 'Let's go and get your bag and have a look at your bedroom.'

I walked out into the hallway expecting to find a bin bag or carrier bags, particularly as it had been so rushed, but there was a large holdall by the front door.

I carried it upstairs and the girls followed me.

'I've got a big girl called Amena staying with me at the moment and that's her room,' I told them, pointing to the other bedroom door. 'So if you hear anybody in the night going to the toilet then that will probably be her.

'And that door there is my bedroom,' I added, pointing down the landing. 'So if you need anything at all in the night, or you're worried or scared, you can shout for me or come and get me.

'And this is the bedroom where you'll be sleeping,' I told them, pushing open the door.

They followed me in nervously but I could see that they were curious.

'Coco, you could sleep on the top bunk if you want and Lola on the bottom?' I suggested.

Coco shook her head.

'I might fall out,' she said.

'That's OK,' I replied. 'There's another bed over there so neither of you need to have the top bunk.'

On each of the beds, I'd put a towel, a toothbrush and a teddy to make them feel more at home. Now they'd put their blankets down, I could see they were both wearing pyjamas. Both pairs were very worn and faded and Coco's were much too small for her – the legs and the sleeves were too short and her belly was peeking out from below the top. But they seemed clean and from where I was stood, I could smell the fresh scent of washing powder.

Their hair needed a brush but it wasn't matted or dirty and their nails were clean and their skin pink and soft. The heating was on so they'd started to warm up and they looked clean and comfortable so I decided that a bath could wait until the morning.

'Shall we go and brush your teeth, girls, and get you into bed?' I said gently.

Coco grabbed her sister's hand.

'Come on, Lola,' she told her in a sweet, almost motherly voice. 'Let's go and do a wee wee and brush our teeth.'

They both knew how to use the toilet and wash their hands without any help from me, then they expertly brushed their own teeth.

Afterwards I took them back to the bedroom and helped them both into bed – Lola had the bottom bunk and Coco had the single bed on the other side of the room. They both lay on their backs, looking around them with wide eyes.

I put on the little lamp that was on top of the chest of drawers and turned the ceiling light off so it was more cosy for them.

'Do you want me to leave that on?' I asked them.

Lola shook her head.

'No, we're used to the dark,' Coco told me.

I tucked each of them in with the teddy that I'd left on the ends of their bed.

'I know it's been a really long, hard day for you both but try to get some sleep and we'll find out more about Mummy in the morning, OK?'

Coco nodded. Lola didn't say a word but let out a loud, rattling cough.

'Do you want a glass of water, lovey?' I asked her but she shook her head.

'I'm going to go downstairs now but if you need me, just shout "Maggie", OK?'

I hoped that they would settle quickly as I could see they were shattered. Often on their first night with me, children did tend to fall into a deep sleep as they were so exhausted after the trauma and the emotion of the day, but I also knew that every child reacted differently.

I turned the landing light on and left the bedroom door ajar. Then I went downstairs and gave my agency a call.

'Janet, just to let you know that the girls are here,' I told her as quietly as I could. 'The social worker's gone and I've just put them to bed.'

'That's good news,' she said. 'I'm glad it wasn't too late. How do they seem?'

'As you'd expect,' I told her. 'Very quiet and bewildered but physically they seem OK. They're clean and they're well-mannered and seem like lovely little girls.'

'We'll hopefully know more in the morning,' she told me. 'I'm sure Social Services will be in touch first thing when they've got an update on Mum.'

After I'd hung up, I did a bit of tidying up and then crept back upstairs. I peeped in through the door. Thankfully Lola was already fast asleep but Coco was still lying on her back, staring at the ceiling.

'Are you OK?' I whispered and she nodded.

'Are you going to work now?' she asked me.

I looked at her, confused.

'No, flower, I'm not going anywhere,' I replied. 'I'll be right here. Remember I showed you my bedroom just down the landing. Try to get some sleep but you can give me a shout anytime that you need me, OK?'

Coco nodded.

'Night night,' I whispered. 'See you in the morning.'

Being left alone at night was clearly something no three- and seven-year-old should be used to but I knew now wasn't the time to be asking questions. There was plenty of time for that.

THREE

Emergency Dash

It was the screams that woke me. High-pitched, blood-curdling screams that made me sit bolt upright in bed with my heart racing.

'Mummy?' yelled the voice. 'Where are you? Are you back from work? Mummy, please come!'

I leapt up out of bed and ran onto the landing. In the darkness, I could just make out a figure standing there.

Coco.

I hadn't had a chance to check the time but it was still pitch black outside and I could tell it was still the middle of the night.

'Mummy!' she screamed again, tears rolling down her cheeks. 'Where did you go? Please come back, Mummy!'

I quickly turned on the landing light. I could see by the blank, glassy expression in Coco's eyes that she was still half asleep. I put my arms around her shoulders, desperate to calm her down and hope that her screams hadn't woken Lola or Amena up.

'Coco, it's Maggie,' I told her gently. 'Remember you're staying at my house tonight? The social worker brought you here earlier.'

She looked up at me, confused.

'Was it you?' she asked. 'Did you take my mummy away?'

'Coco, your mummy is talking to the police,' I reminded her. 'They've taken her to the police station to answer a few questions. It's the middle of the night now but tomorrow I'll be able to talk to your social worker and find out more about where your mummy is.'

Coco's face crumpled and tears spilled out of her eyes.

'But I want my mummy now,' she sobbed. 'She's at work. She'll be back soon.'

'Coco, your mum is with the police,' I repeated. 'And I'll do my best to make sure that you see her or speak to her very soon. I know this is so scary and confusing for you and Lola, but Mummy is OK, I promise you.'

Coco blinked back the tears.

'It's still the middle of the night, flower,' I soothed. 'And I don't want Lola to wake up so let's get you tucked back into bed. You'll feel much better if you get some sleep and then when you wake up in the morning, we can find out more about your mummy, OK?'

Coco nodded, but I could tell that she was still groggy with sleep and very confused.

I gently led her back into the bedroom where she and Lola were sleeping. As she got into bed and pulled the duvet over herself, across the room Lola stirred in her sleep and let out a loud, rattly cough. I held my breath but thankfully it didn't seem to disturb her and she settled again. But the same couldn't be said for Coco.

She couldn't seem to get comfy and she was thrashing around.

'Mummy,' she murmured. 'Mummy, I'll come and find you.'

I knelt on the floor next to her bed and stroked her wispy blonde hair.

'It's OK,' I soothed. 'We'll find out more about Mummy tomorrow.'

I had to keep repeating the same things because that's all I knew myself at this early stage.

'Sleep tight, Coco,' I whispered. 'I'm just down the landing if you need me again.'

But she didn't respond and it was a relief to see that her eyes were finally closed and at last she was still.

As I padded back down the landing to my bedroom, I prayed that she would stay settled. I picked up my phone to check the time. It was 3.30 a.m.

Down the hall, I heard Lola coughing again.

It had taken what felt like ages for me to fall back to sleep and now I was wide awake, my mind racing, thinking of the two little girls in my spare room and wondering what the following day was going to bring. The first few days of a new placement were always strange, getting to know the children and them getting to know me and working out what the situation was. It often took days or even weeks for information to filter through from Social Services. It was like doing a jigsaw – waiting for all of the pieces so you could begin piecing them together.

Judging by the silence, Coco had thankfully drifted off into a deep sleep but I couldn't. Every time I was about to nod off, I'd hear Lola coughing and I was suddenly wide awake again. Thankfully it didn't seem to disturb her but I made a mental note to take her to the GP and get it checked out if it persisted.

Eventually I must have got some sleep but it felt like my eyes had only just closed when I heard someone shouting.

'Abbie,' a voice yelled. 'Abbie. Please can you come now?'

It was Coco and she sounded scared.

I leapt out of bed and ran out onto the landing. This time it was just getting light. Coco looked up at me with worried green eyes.

'Please can you help me,' she whimpered. 'There's something wrong with my sister.'

Her words chilled me to the bone and I didn't even have the chance to correct her and tell her that my name was Maggie, not Abbie. I dashed into the bedroom and went over to Lola in the bottom bunk. Her eyes were closed but she was moaning and I could see that she was shivering. Her blonde hair was soaked in sweat and plastered to her forehead, and her lips had a grey tinge about them. I quickly felt her forehead – she was burning up.

'What's wrong with her?' asked Coco.

'I don't know, sweetie,' I told her.

As if on cue, Lola let out a rattly cough. I put my hand on her chest and I could feel and see that her breathing was shallow and laboured. Every time she took a breath, the muscles under her ribcage sucked inwards.

There was something horribly wrong.

'Has she had that cough a long time?' I asked Coco and she nodded.

'Mummy was going to the shop to get her some medicine,' she told me.

30

I didn't know anything about Lola's medical history but instinct told me she was really poorly. She was lethargic and struggling to breathe and I wasn't prepared to take any chances. I knew I needed to get her to the hospital – and quick.

In my head I ran through everything I needed to do to get Lola to A&E. I could call for an ambulance but the wait could potentially be hours. I knew it would be quicker to drive her to the hospital myself.

I glanced at the little clock that was on the bedside table next to Lola's bed. It was 6 a.m. and Amena was still fast asleep. She normally got up around 7 a.m. and left the house to get the bus to school an hour later. She was old enough to get herself dressed and ready and leave the house, but what was I going to do with Coco? Ideally, I didn't want to take her to A&E with me as we'd potentially be waiting around for hours.

'You sit with Lola for two minutes,' I told Coco. 'I'm just going to make a very quick phone call.'

I ran back to my room, grabbed my mobile and sat on the bed. It was very early but I prayed Louisa was already awake.

It only rang a couple of times before she picked up.

'Maggie?' she asked, her voice filled with concern. 'Is everything OK?'

'Sorry to bother you at this time of the morning,' I replied.

'Oh don't worry, we've been up ages,' she told me. 'You know what an early riser Edie is. We've already had breakfast and she's watching TV now. But what is it? You sound stressed.'

I explained that the two girls had arrived late last night.

'They've just woken up and Lola – the three-year-old – is very poorly,' I told her. 'Her breathing is really rapid and shallow and she's burning up. I don't want to take any chances so I think I need to take her straight to A&E. But obviously I'm a bit stuck as I've got her older sister Coco here as well.'

'Maggie, don't worry,' Louisa told me calmly. 'I can take Coco for you.'

'Are you sure?' I asked her. 'I know you've got work today.'

Louisa was a nanny for a local family. They had a four-year-old boy who was at school now and another little boy who was the same age as Edie. It worked out well as Louisa was able to take Edie to work with her.

'I'll drop Liz a quick message but I'm sure she won't mind,' she told me. 'It's an emergency and she knows all about your fostering. She's always talking about how amazing you are to do what you do.'

I'd met Liz – the mum of the two boys – a couple of times and she seemed like a nice woman. Liz and her family had treated Louisa well over the years. She'd started working for them when their eldest was a baby and she had talked to them about how I'd taken her in as a teenager when her parents had died.

'Thanks so much, lovey,' I told her.

I knew Coco was unsettled as it was and it was going to be even more traumatic for her to see me take her sister away but at least I was leaving her in safe hands. If anyone could comfort and reassure her, it was Louisa.

'Why don't Edie and I get in the car now and come round to you and you can introduce me to Coco?' she told me. 'It will give you a chance to get ready. We can stay at your house for a bit. I'll make sure Amena gets off to school OK and then I can go straight to work.'

'That would be amazing,' I told her.

'I'm so grateful for your help,' I sighed. 'What would I do without you?'

'Maggie, you help me and Charlie out all the time with Edie,' she said. 'After everything you've done for me over the years, it's nice that I can return the favour for once.'

I quickly filled her in on what I knew so far about Coco.

'I actually know very little,' I told her. 'The girls haven't even been assigned a social worker yet.'

I explained how last night she'd seen her mum being taken away by the police.

'Then she was brought by a stranger to my house and now I'm taking her sister away and leaving her with someone else she doesn't know.'

'Poor little mite,' sighed Louisa. 'I'll be there for cuddles and reassurance if she needs them.'

'Thank you,' I said. 'I'd better go now and check on the girls but see you soon.'

I put the phone down and dashed back into the bedroom, where Coco was sitting on the bed stroking Lola's hair. I could see that Lola's breathing was still very rapid and laboured and she was feverish.

I knelt on the floor next to Coco.

'I'm going to take Lola to see a doctor so they can give her some medicine for her nasty cough,' I told her calmly. I didn't want to say that I was taking her to the hospital as I didn't want to worry her even more.

'But Mummy said she would get the medicine from the shop,' Coco told me.

'Your mummy's still talking to the police, sweetie,' I explained. 'So I'm going to get the medicine instead. We might have to wait a long, long time to see the doctor so my lovely big girl, Louisa, is going to come round and look after you while we're gone.'

She looked confused.

'A big girl?' she questioned. 'Is she ten?'

'No, she's much older than that,' I explained. 'Louisa's a grown-up and she's got her own little girl. You'll meet her as well. Her name is Edie and she's two.'

'Like Lola,' she nodded.

'Almost,' I smiled. 'But your sister's a little bit older.'

I explained that Louisa and Edie were on their way over to the house.

'I want to get you some breakfast before I go and Amena will be awake soon so I'll introduce you to her.'

Coco looked confused. She'd obviously already forgotten about me telling her about Amena the night before.

'Amena's another big girl,' I told her. 'She's fifteen and she lives with me at the moment.'

We went downstairs and I got her settled at the kitchen table then I dashed back upstairs to get Lola. I was so worried about her; there was no way I was going to leave her upstairs on her own. She was coughing and thrashing around when I went back into the bedroom.

'I'm going to take you downstairs now, flower, so I can keep an eye on you,' I told her.

As gently as possible, I lifted Lola out of bed. She hardly weighed a thing so I managed to cradle her little body in my arms like a baby as well as grab a pillow.

Slowly and carefully, I carried her downstairs, watching every step to make sure that Lola was OK and there was no chance of me falling.

Lola was in no fit state to sit up. I had a sofa by the patio doors in the kitchen so I gently laid her down on it and put the pillow underneath her head. I had a snuggly fleece blanket that I kept over the back of the sofa so I put it over Lola to keep her warm. Even though she was burning up, she was still shivering with cold and she had another coughing fit.

Coco looked over anxiously from where she was sitting at the kitchen table.

'It's OK,' I told her. 'I'm going to get her some medicine now and that will help until we're able to see the doctor.'

I went over to the high cupboard where I kept all of my medications and got out a bottle of Calpol and a little plastic syringe. Then I got a beaker of water with a straw.

I took them over to Lola and crouched on the floor next to the sofa. Her eyes suddenly opened and she looked at me groggily.

'Lola, sweetie, I'm going to give you some medicine to try to cool you down a bit,' I told her.

She didn't say anything but thankfully she let me squirt a syringe full of Calpol into the corner of her mouth.

'Have a few sips of this please,' I said, holding the beaker and straw next to her.

She managed to lift her head slightly and take three or four little sips before she collapsed down on the pillow again and closed her eyes.

'Good girl,' I soothed. 'That's going to make you feel a lot better.'

I walked back over to Coco.

'Right, let's get you some breakfast now,' I smiled. 'You must be starving.'

A lot of children in the care system who come to live with me don't know how to sit and eat at a table but while I'd been seeing to Lola, Coco had sat there very patiently. I put some boxes of cereal on the table as well as a jug of milk and a bowl and spoon.

'Thank you,' she said politely.

She poured herself a big bowl of cornflakes, carefully poured the milk on and tucked in. I could see she was starving; she couldn't get the cereal into her mouth quick enough.

'If you're still hungry then I can make you some toast?' I told her and she nodded.

'Would you like a glass of orange juice?'

'Yes please,' she nodded.

As I was making breakfast for Coco, I kept one eye on Lola at all times. She kept on moaning and violently coughing and I could see the worried look on Coco's face.

'She's going to be OK,' I reassured her. 'Louisa will be here any minute and I'll take her straight to see the doctor.'

Coco nodded.

Just then, I heard footsteps on the stairs and Amena walked into the kitchen dressed in her school uniform.

'Oh, hello, flower,' I smiled. 'I didn't realise you were up.'

Coco stared at Amena shyly.

'This is Coco,' I told her. 'She's seven, and she and her sister Lola arrived late last night.'

'Hi, Coco,' she grinned. 'I'm Amena.'

Coco gave her a shy smile and got back to carefully eating

her cereal. Amena suddenly noticed Lola lying on the sofa.

'What's wrong with the other little girl?' she asked.

I explained in a quiet voice that Lola wasn't very well.

'I thought I heard coughing in the night,' she nodded.

'Louisa's on her way over now with Edie and she's going to take Coco to work with her while I take Lola to the hospital.'

'What's the matter with her?' Amena asked anxiously.

'I don't know yet,' I said. 'She's got a fever and a bad cough and just to be on the safe side, I want to get her checked out. Are you OK to get yourself to school as normal?'

Amena nodded.

'Good girl,' I told her. 'I'm sure we'll be back by the time you get home this afternoon.'

Amena was such a kind, adaptable girl. She'd only been with me a few weeks but she never moaned or complained about anything.

Suddenly Lola let out the most horrific chesty cough. She was coughing so much, I was worried she was about to be sick. Amena and Coco looked alarmed as I ran over to her.

I managed to prop her up on her pillow and give her a few sips of water until she finally got her breath back.

'Good girl,' I soothed, bathing her forehead with a wet flannel.

I glanced up at the clock on my kitchen wall.

Come on Louisa, I thought to myself. *Please hurry up.*

Adrenalin coursed through me and I swallowed the panic rising up in my throat.

Despite the Calpol, I could see Lola was deteriorating right in front of me. All of my instincts were screaming at me that I needed to get her to the hospital – and fast.

FOUR

Seeking Help

It was such a relief when, a few minutes later, I heard a car pull up outside.

That has to be Louisa, I told myself as I ran to the front door.

As soon as I opened it, Edie came tearing up the path towards me. Her cheeks were all rosy in the early morning frost and she was dressed in a cute pair of denim dungarees that I'd bought her and a little pink coat.

'Nana!' she grinned, throwing her arms around my legs.

'Hello, sweetheart,' I smiled, bending down to give her a hug. 'Ooh, your little hands are freezing.'

Despite my worry over Lola and how early it was, seeing Edie's cheery little face never failed to lift my spirits.

'I wish I was as chirpy as her at this time of the morning,' said a tired-looking Louisa, trudging up the path behind her.

Her hair was still wet and she had no make-up on.

'Thank you so much for this,' I told her.

'How's Lola?' she asked.

'Not great,' I replied. 'She's floppy and lethargic and still struggling to breathe. I'm really worried about her.'

'You'll feel better when you get her checked over at the hospital,' Louisa told me.

I knew she was right.

I took Louisa into the front room where Coco was sitting on the sofa watching a cartoon on TV.

'Coco, this is Louisa – my big girl who I was telling you all about,' I explained. 'She's going to look after you while I take Lola to see the doctor.'

Coco looked up at her with those anxious green eyes.

'Hi, Coco,' smiled Louisa. 'My daughter Edie was looking forward to meeting you,' she said. 'But she's gone straight through to the kitchen because she knows that's where Nana keeps the toys! Do you want to come and say hello to her?'

Coco nodded and quietly followed her through to the kitchen.

Edie had already thrown open the toy cupboard and was rummaging through it while Amena had her breakfast at the table. Lola was now fast asleep on the sofa.

'Oh, bless her,' sighed Louisa. 'Hi, Amena,' she smiled.

Coco went over to where Edie was playing and sat down on the floor next to her, watching closely as she roughly brushed a doll's hair with a plastic brush that she'd found.

'She seems fine, Maggie,' Louisa told me in a quiet voice. 'Why don't you go and get ready and I'll keep an eye on them?'

I looked down and remembered that I was still in my dressing gown. I hadn't even brushed my teeth yet.

'Thanks, lovey,' I said.

I went over to Lola and felt her clammy forehead. Thankfully the Calpol seemed to have finally taken effect and she was a lot more settled. I still wanted to get her to the hospital as quickly as possible so I ran upstairs to get ready. I splashed some water on my face and pulled on some jeans and a jumper. I dashed round the house putting a few essentials in a bag – water, some snacks, my phone charger and the delegated responsibility forms that thankfully the duty social worker, Arti, had given me the previous night, which meant I had permission to seek medical help for Lola.

I ran back downstairs. Everything still seemed calm in the kitchen. Amena was almost ready to leave for school and Coco and Edie were playing on the floor while Louisa was putting the kettle on to make a cup of tea. Lola was still fast asleep.

'Do you want one?' she asked me.

'No thanks, lovey,' I said. 'I'm going to get off now.'

'She seems like a sweet girl,' she told me in a quiet voice, gesturing towards Coco. 'She's got lovely manners and she knows how to do imaginative play.'

Many children who came into the care system didn't know how to play. When they were exposed to abusive or neglectful care, often their play development was affected and they struggled to play imaginatively or independently.

'Yes,' I nodded. 'I noticed that too.'

My next challenge was getting Lola from the house to the car. I hated disturbing her when she'd finally settled but I knew I needed to get her to the hospital.

'Lola,' I said, gently shaking her awake. 'I'm going to take you to see a doctor.'

She opened her eyes and looked at me groggily.

'Come on, flower,' I soothed, lifting her off the sofa and onto my knee. I'd decided to leave her in her pyjamas so I pulled a fleecy hoodie that I'd found in my cupboard over her head and wrapped her in the fleecy blanket.

'I'm going to carry you to the car now,' I told her.

She didn't utter a sound as I picked her up and carried her out into the hallway. Louisa had opened the front door and was standing outside by my car with the back door open.

She helped me to lower Lola onto the back seat and she held her up while I put the seatbelt over her and clicked it into place.

As soon as I closed the car door, she slumped to one side, her head resting against the window.

'Can you stay with her for one sec while I go and say bye to the girls?' I asked and Louisa nodded.

I dashed back into the house and through to the kitchen.

'Coco, I'm taking Lola to see the doctor now,' I told her.

'Is she coming back?' she asked.

'Of course she is,' I reassured her. 'You're going to go with Louisa and I will call her and let her know what's happening.'

'What about Mummy?' she asked.

'Remember that Mummy was going to talk to the police people so I will make a few phone calls this morning and see if she has finished chatting and I will let you know. You're such a brave girl and we will see you soon.'

I said a quick goodbye to Amena and gave Edie a hug and then rushed back out to the car where Lola was still dozing in the back.

'Are you going to be all right when you get to the hospital?' asked Louisa. 'How will you manage?'

'I'm hoping that because it's so early, there'll be space in the car park. Besides, she's not really heavy,' I told her.

'Well, call me if you need anything,' she said.

'I will do,' I replied. 'And thanks again, lovey. I'll keep you updated.'

I was so grateful that the nearest hospital with an A&E was only a fifteen-minute drive away from my house. I kept glancing in the rear-view mirror to check Lola was OK. Her eyes were still closed and she kept coughing from time to time, but she was still sleeping,

Thankfully when I pulled into the hospital car park just before 8 a.m., there was one space free. I knew it was going to cost me a fortune but I needed to be as close as possible. It was a cold morning so I clicked Lola's seatbelt off, pulled the blanket back round her and lifted her up.

She groaned and coughed again as I hoisted her onto my hip.

'It's OK, lovey,' I soothed. 'We're here now. Let's get you inside.'

I carried her across the car park and through the doors of the A&E. Even though it was early, it was already a hive of activity with ambulances pulling up, medical staff coming and going, and people in hospital gowns sitting in wheelchairs talking on their phones or having a cigarette outside. I'd been here many times over the past few years and thankfully there was a designated paediatric A&E. I walked through the main emergency department and someone buzzed me in to the paediatric area. The receptionist saw me walking towards her with a groggy Lola draped over my shoulder.

'Are you OK there?' she asked. 'Let me get someone to come and help.'

'Thank you,' I said. 'She doesn't weigh much but my arm is starting to go numb.'

She got up and went into the office behind the reception desk.

'You're in luck for once,' she smiled.

A few seconds later, a porter came out of a side door, pushing a wheelchair.

'That was good timing,' he said cheerfully. 'I've just come off my break.'

'Thanks,' I said as he expertly helped me lower Lola into it.

I needed to get Lola booked in as soon as possible. It was a triage system so they decided which were the most urgent cases who needed to see the doctor first.

The receptionist started to log Lola's details onto the computer.

'Is there any Social Services involvement?' she asked.

'Yes,' I nodded. 'Lola and her older sister have just been taken into the care system and I'm their foster carer. They only arrived at my house last night so I have no history about them really other than what's on this form.'

I showed her the delegated responsibility form, which thankfully had Lola's date of birth on it.

'And what are her symptoms?' she asked.

I explained what had happened and she typed them into the system.

'OK,' she said. 'Take a seat but I expect that they'll want to bring her straight through.'

'Thank you,' I said.

Lola had fallen back to sleep again and it worried me that she was so lethargic. For once, A&E was quiet and there was only a handful of other people waiting – a couple with a young baby in a car seat and an older teenager on crutches who was with her mum.

Around five minutes later, a doctor came out and called Lola's name.

'She's here,' I gestured, getting up off the plastic chair.

'I'm Dr Musa,' she said. 'Let's get her through here and take a look at her.'

I wheeled Lola through a set of double doors and the doctor led us to a cubicle and pulled the curtains around it. She helped me lift Lola out of the wheelchair and lay her gently on the bed. I sat in the chair next to the bed and explained her symptoms.

'She's lethargic and floppy and her breathing is really laboured,' I explained. 'She only arrived at my house last night and I don't have any further information about her long-term health. But given her age and her symptoms, I didn't want to take any chances. It scared me when I saw how she was this morning. She's coughing a lot and when she breathes in, it's like her ribcage is sucking inwards.'

'You did the right thing bringing her in,' Dr Musa nodded. 'I'm going to take her temperature and listen to her chest, do an ECG and probably take some bloods. We might want to do a chest X-ray too.'

Lola was still very floppy and sleepy.

'Lola, I'm Dr Musa,' she said in a loud voice as she gently unwrapped the blanket from her. 'I'm going to put you in a hospital gown now so it's easier to have a look at you.'

Lola moaned.

'Mummy,' she said.

The doctor looked at me.

'Lola, Mummy's still talking to the police but she will come and see you soon,' I told her.

'Am I OK to quickly nip out and make a few phone calls?' I asked the nurse who was helping Dr Musa. 'I really need to let Social Services know what's happening.'

'Of course,' she said. 'We're just going to get her comfortable and then we'll do a few tests.'

It was still early but I knew I needed to let my agency know what was happening so they could pass the information on to Social Services.

I knew Becky, my supervising social worker, normally got to the office before 9 a.m. so I called her mobile. She picked up straight away.

'Morning, Maggie,' she said cheerfully. 'Janet's filled me in on what happened last night. Did the girls arrive OK and can you send me copies of the paperwork?'

I paused.

'Maggie,' she asked. 'Is everything OK?'

'Not really,' I said. 'I'm ringing you from the hospital.'

I explained what had happened.

'Gosh, poor kid,' she said. 'And what a scare for you. How's she doing now?'

'The doctor is with her now doing some tests,' I told her.

I explained that I'd had no other option but to leave Coco with Louisa.

'Understandably, Coco's very anxious and wants to know what's happening with her mum.'

'Of course,' replied Becky. 'When I get off the phone to you, I'll give Social Services a call. They'll probably appoint a social worker later on today. As soon as I know anything I'll give you a ring,' she told me. 'But please keep me updated on Lola.'

'Will do,' I told her.

I also gave Louisa a quick call.

'Everything's fine,' she reassured me. 'I've spoken to Liz and she's happy for me to bring Coco with me today so we're about to drive over there now. How's Lola doing?' she asked.

'The doctor's just with her now,' I said. 'In fact I'd better go and see how she's getting on.'

I went back into A&E and through to paediatrics. Dr Musa was still examining Lola.

'I'm afraid it looks very likely that she's got pneumonia,' she told me.

'Pneumonia?' I gasped.

'She's very dehydrated so I'm going to put her on some fluids and antibiotics via a drip,' she replied. 'She's obviously been sick for a fair few days – it's a good job you brought her in when you did,' she added. 'Children can sometimes start going downhill very quickly.'

It was relief to know what was wrong but it was a lot more serious than I'd hoped.

'Will she have to stay in?' I asked.

'Definitely,' nodded Dr Musa. 'We need to keep a close eye on her over the next few days and get her vitals more stable.'

After an hour or so they wheeled Lola down to a children's ward. Thankfully she seemed a lot more settled but every so often she would cough violently and call out for her mummy.

'You'll see Mummy soon,' I tried to reassure her.

A nurse, a middle-aged Irish woman who had just come on duty, looked at me quizzically.

'Are you Nana?' she asked.

'I'm actually her foster carer,' I explained.

'Oh, I see,' she said. 'Have you had her long?'

'She and her sister only arrived last night,' I told her. 'So she hasn't even been with me for twenty-four hours yet.'

'Poor little lass,' she sighed, shaking her head. 'Why did she get taken into care then?'

Throughout all my years of fostering, it never ceases to amaze me that strangers think it's OK to ask me why a child that I'm looking after has been taken into care. I'm always very vague and explain that children come into care for all sorts of reasons and it can be something as simple as their parent is a single parent and they've had to go into hospital. I am not offended by it because I know people aren't deliberately being rude, it's just a natural curiosity. However, what does bother me is when people ask that question when the child is with me. On those occasions I say, 'I'm sorry I can't talk about that' and I quickly move away. It's important for the child to know I'm not going to talk about them and disclose any personal information about them to strangers.

Thankfully Lola wasn't 'with it' enough to have heard what the nurse had just asked me.

'I'm afraid I'm not allowed to discuss individual cases,' I told her.

'Oh, I am sorry,' she replied, her cheeks flushing red. 'I understand. I was just being nosy.'

'That's OK,' I smiled, not wanting her to feel bad. 'You're not the first person to ask that question and you won't be the last. The poor little mite probably doesn't even remember who I am. So if she asks then feel free to remind her that I'm Maggie.'

'I will do,' the nurse nodded.

I thought back to Coco this morning who probably still thought that I was called Abbie.

'I think what you do is amazing,' the nurse added as she checked Lola's temperature. 'I don't know how you do it though. I know I couldn't bear to give them back.'

Now that was a remark I also found irritating. I hated the assumption that if you were a foster carer then you didn't have any feelings about children moving on. The implication was that you were quite hard-nosed and not affected, but that couldn't be further from the truth. As a foster carer, you always feel such a deep sense of loss when a child leaves and in private I had cried buckets of tears over the years. I was affected by every single child who left my care although you might not know that to look at me. It's not that I didn't care, I just had to develop coping strategies to protect myself and accept that it was part and parcel of fostering. I had to say goodbye in order to enable that child to move on.

'It's always very hard,' I told the nurse. 'But you learn that it's just part of the job.'

I looked at Lola lying in her hospital bed and sighed. She looked so small and vulnerable and I wished I could do more to help her. I knew nothing about her and her sister yet and what they'd been through, and there was still so much to find out. It had been the strangest start to a placement but hopefully things would start to improve from here.

FIVE

Calm After the Storm

The rest of the morning was spent sitting on an uncomfortable plastic chair by Lola's bed. She'd mainly been sleeping since we got here, only opening her eyes very occasionally when she was disturbed by a coughing fit. All I could hope was that the antibiotics and fluids were doing their job.

'You're going to be OK, Lola,' I reassured her as her eyes flickered open and then promptly closed again.

I wondered what on earth she must be thinking in that little head of hers.

Even though I was reassured that she was in the right place, I felt so helpless. There was nothing useful I could do but I wanted to be there in case she woke up and became distressed or frightened. Even though she didn't actually know me, I didn't want her to feel that she was all alone.

At the same time, I felt incredibly guilty for leaving Coco only hours after she'd arrived at my house. Louisa had texted a few times to say that she was absolutely fine but I still couldn't help but worry about how upsetting this must be for her too.

Just after 11 a.m. my mobile rang. It was a withheld number.

'Hello, is that Maggie?' asked a well-spoken voice.

'It is,' I replied. 'How can I help you?'

'It's Pamela Griggs from Social Services,' she said. 'I've been appointed as Coco and Lola's social worker.'

'Oh, hi,' I told her. 'To be honest, I didn't expect a call until this afternoon. I'm actually just at the hospital with Lola now.'

'I'm sorry to hear that she's so poorly,' she said.

'Yes, she gave me quite the scare this morning,' I replied. 'But she seems to be doing OK now, although she's sleeping a lot.'

She explained that she'd like to come up to the hospital and meet me and Lola.

'That's fine, Pam,' I told her. 'I'm probably going to be here for most of the day.'

'Actually it's Pamela, not Pam,' she said abruptly.

'Oh I am sorry,' I said, slightly taken aback by the annoyed tone of her voice.

'I've got a meeting now but I'll head over to the hospital in an hour, so I'll see you then,' she said before hanging up.

I hadn't worked with Pamela before but she had a very bristly manner about her. I hoped that I'd got the wrong impression and that she was much warmer and friendlier in person.

The rest of the morning passed slowly. The nurse who I'd been talking to earlier came in occasionally to check on Lola.

'She's been asleep for hours,' I sighed. 'Is that normal?'

'Try not to worry. It's her body's way of recovering,' she smiled. 'She's doing much better than she was and her fever has gone down – the doctor will come and check on her later.'

'Thank you,' I smiled. 'I think I'm still living on my nerves from the dash to hospital this morning.'

Feeling more reassured, I decided to go for a walk to stretch my legs. I went down to the hospital lobby and got a cardboard-tasting sandwich and a thick, sickly sweet hot chocolate from the café that I brought back to the cubicle. I was just texting Becky to update her when I heard heels click-clacking down the corridor and suddenly the curtain around the bed was pulled back.

'Hello, Maggie?' asked a voice.

I turned around to see a woman in her fifties, in black trousers, a patterned blouse and a grey waterfall cardigan. She had bobbed ashy-blonde hair and a pair of blue glasses hanging around her neck on a gold chain.

'Maggie?' she asked, flashing me her Social Services lanyard. 'I'm Pamela from Social Services.'

She reached out her hand to me and I shook it.

'Pleased to meet you,' I said, forcibly reminding myself not to call her Pam.

'And this must be Lola,' she sighed, walking over to the bed.

'It is,' I smiled. 'Poor thing has been asleep for hours. But the doctor is pleased – she's much more settled and her temperature has gone right down. She's still coughing but it's a lot less than earlier.'

'That's good,' she nodded. 'And where's her sister?'

I explained who Louisa was and that Coco was with her.

'I'm a single carer and Louisa is my support person,' I told her.

You can't have sole responsibility for a foster child unless you are twenty-one. Louisa had grown up around foster children in my house, so as soon as she had turned twenty-one, she had been police-checked, assessed and approved by my agency, which meant that she could step in and look after any of my foster children both overnight and in the day. She could also undergo any of the training that foster carers had access to. My other support person was my friend Vicky, who was a fellow foster carer so she'd already had all of the necessary checks.

'Have you managed to speak to the girls' mum?' I asked.

'No, I haven't spoken to Zoe yet,' Pamela told me. 'The police released her late last night and she's back at the flat, I believe. One of my colleagues spoke to her this morning to let her know that Lola was in hospital.'

'Poor woman,' I sighed. 'It must have been such a shock to hear that.'

'I think it was,' nodded Pamela. 'We said we'd arrange for her to come up to the hospital to see Lola later on today but I wanted to speak to you about it first. Obviously a hospital visit is OK as I'll be here, so she'll be fully supervised.'

Contact was always supervised when any child first came into care. It was a way for Social Services to get an immediate insight into how children responded to the parent/s and how the parent/s responded to them.

Pamela said she would arrange to bring Zoe to the hospital between 5 and 6 p.m. that afternoon.

'With all due respect, Maggie, I would rather you weren't here then,' she told me. 'We don't know how Mum is going to react to seeing you.'

'Of course,' I nodded. 'I completely understand. I can nip home and do tea for the girls.'

I didn't want any potential conflict on the hospital ward and in front of Lola. It was going to be hard enough for Zoe to see her daughter so poorly without seeing me there as well.

'What about Coco?' I asked. 'She's desperate to see her mum too and she'll be distraught if she knows that she's visited Lola.'

'I understand,' nodded Pamela. 'I'm going to set up a session at a contact centre as soon as I can. Hopefully I can get something sorted for tomorrow but I think that's probably being over-optimistic.'

The contact centres were often so busy it could take a few days to find an available slot in the local area.

'And what are you going to do overnight?' asked Pamela. 'Are you going to stay at the hospital or are you planning on going home?'

I'd been agonising over this all day. I didn't want Lola to wake up in hospital alone and be upset. But at the same time, she was still very groggy and sleeping a lot and, in a way, Coco needed me more. I wanted to be there to reassure her that her sister was going to be OK. Also, there was Amena to think about and I didn't know if Louisa was able to drop everything and stay overnight at my house. She'd already done so much for me today.

'I think I'll need to go home,' I told her. 'Coco needs that reassurance and I have another placement at the moment too.'

Pamela nodded.

'I'll make sure the ward nurse has my number and I'll call later on tonight for an update and come back first thing in the morning,' I said.

There was also something else I'd been thinking about that I needed to run by Pamela.

'What should I do about Coco and school?' I asked.

'I think let's not worry about school this week,' she replied. 'As I haven't spoken to Mum yet, we don't even know which school she goes to or even if she was attending school. There's so much going on with Lola being in hospital so let's give Coco a bit of time to try to settle in and work out what's happening.'

I nodded. It felt like the right decision and certainly made life easier for me.

'Well, I'm going to go now, Maggie, as I have a meeting back in town but it was nice to meet you,' said Pamela, giving my hand a vigorous shake. 'I'll bring Zoe here later on to see Lola and then we can touch base again in the morning.'

'No problem,' I nodded.

Pamela grabbed her handbag and left, her heels clacking on the ward floor. I honestly didn't know what to make of her and her cold, business-like manner.

I spent the next few hours at Lola's bedside. But as the afternoon wore on, I knew I needed to leave so I didn't risk running into Pamela and Zoe.

Lola looked very settled but I felt guilty.

'She'll be fine,' said the nurse, whose name I'd found out was Sorcha. 'Her temperature has gone down further and those antibiotics are kicking in. We've got our eyes on her – you go home to your other kids.'

'Thank you,' I said. 'The ward sister has my number in case of any problem.'

I still felt incredibly guilty as I packed my bag up and prepared to leave the hospital.

'Bye, flower,' I whispered to Lola and patted her hand. 'Mummy's coming to see you soon and I'll see you again tomorrow.'

The sun was close to setting as I walked across the car park and I could tell it was going to be another cold night. I felt groggy after spending most of the day inside under the sterile lights of the ward.

Please let her be OK, I said to myself as I headed home.

When I pushed open my front door, twenty minutes later, I was greeted by a delicious smell.

'Hello!' I shouted as I took my coat off.

A few seconds later Edie came running out to me.

'Nana back,' she grinned.

'Yes, Nana's back,' I smiled.

I walked through to the kitchen where Louisa was taking a bubbling pasta bake out of the oven.

'Oh, wow,' I sighed. 'You didn't have to do that, lovey.'

'Liz let me go early and I wasn't sure how long you'd be so I thought I'd make some tea for the girls.'

'How are they?' I asked.

She explained that Amena was upstairs doing her homework and Coco was in the front room watching TV.

'I must have walked right past her,' I said. 'How's she been?'

'Good as gold,' said Louisa. 'She's had a couple of teary moments but considering what she's been through in the past twenty-four hours, she's doing amazingly well.'

'I'll go and say hello to her,' I replied.

I walked back into the hallway and into the front room. Coco was glued to the TV but she looked up expectantly when I came in. Her face fell when she saw I was on my own.

'Where's Lola?' she asked.

I sat down next to her on the sofa.

'I took Lola to see the doctor,' I explained. 'And the doctor wanted her to go to the hospital so she could have some special medicine to make her feel better.'

I could see the worry in Coco's eyes.

'The doctor wants Lola to stay in the hospital for a little bit while the medicine starts working.'

Coco nodded.

'Will she be there for a long, long time?' she asked.

'Hopefully not,' I told her. 'Once the special medicine starts to work then the doctors will let her come home. Would you like me to take you to the hospital tomorrow so you can see her?'

Coco nodded eagerly.

'What about Mummy?' she asked 'Can I see her too?'

'I know you want to see Mummy so we're going to try to make that happen as soon we can, but she won't be there tomorrow.'

I could see how disappointed Coco was but there wasn't much else I could say to reassure her at this point as I didn't know when Pamela would be able to find space at a contact centre.

A few minutes later, Louisa shouted that dinner was ready. Coco's eyes widened as Louisa put down steaming plates of pasta bake in front of her and Amena.

'Wow!' Coco gasped. 'That's a lot and it's so hot. Thank you.' She seemed so grateful as she tucked in enthusiastically.

Once again, I was struck by her lovely manners and how nicely she used her knife and fork. 'What do you normally have at home?' I asked her.

Coco shrugged.

'Whatever Mummy gets. Bread or crisps or cereal or sometimes biscuits,' she told me. 'Not like this. Mummy says our cooker is broken.'

After dinner, I snuck off upstairs to ring the hospital and then call Becky to update her.

The ward sister on duty reassured me that Lola was comfortable and that the doctor was pleased with her progress.

Then I rang Becky.

'Lola's got to stay in hospital at least for tonight,' I told her.

'Poor girl,' she sighed.

'I've come home to look after Coco but the ward have got my number and they've said she's settled and comfortable.'

I explained that I wanted to take Coco to the hospital in the morning to visit Lola.

'First she watched her mum being taken by the police and now her sister's disappeared,' I said. 'I can see that she's very scared and anxious so I want her to see for herself that her sister's safe.'

Ideally I wanted to leave at 9 a.m. after Amena had gone to school.

'I'm not sure I'll get hold of Pamela, their social worker, in time in the morning so I just wanted to run it by you and check that it's OK.'

'I think that sounds like a good plan,' agreed Becky. 'Coco needs that reassurance; she needs to see her sister.'

It was good to have her backing.

'I hope you manage to get a good night's sleep,' she told me.

'So do I,' I replied.

I said goodbye to Becky and when I'd hung up, I lay back on my bed and closed my eyes for a minute.

The last twenty-four hours had really taken it out of me and suddenly I felt exhausted.

But no matter what I felt, I knew it wasn't a patch on how poor Coco and Lola must be feeling. There was no perfect way for a child to come into the care system but the past twenty-four hours had been heartbreaking, frightening and stressful for both of them. All I could hope was that the next few days were calm and settled and that we could start to get more of an idea about them and their home life and what we were dealing with.

SIX

Visiting Time

By 7 p.m., I could see Edie was getting tired so I waved Louisa off.

'You look shattered too, Maggie,' she told me as I helped Edie get her coat on in the hallway.

'I must admit, I am a bit,' I said. 'I sat down on my bed earlier to make a phone call and honestly I felt like nodding off. I think Coco is done in as well so I'm going to give her a bath and then I think both of us will head straight to bed.

'Thanks again for helping out today,' I added. 'I don't know what I'd do without you.'

'It wasn't a problem,' Louisa said. 'Do you need me to look after Coco tomorrow? I'm sure Liz wouldn't mind if I took her to work with me again.'

I explained that I was hoping to take her up to the hospital first thing in the morning so she could see Lola.

'I think she'd really appreciate that,' nodded Louisa. 'You can tell she's really anxious about her sister.'

Hopefully over the next few days we'd find out more about what was happening with Zoe. I didn't even know at this stage if the police had charged her with anything. For all we knew, it might have all been a misunderstanding.

I also wondered how her visit to the hospital to see Lola had gone that evening. I wouldn't find out any of this until I spoke to Pamela in the morning.

Once Louisa and Edie had left, I went into the front room where Coco was slumped on the sofa. She had a tired, glassy look in her eyes and I could tell that she was exhausted.

'Come on, Coco,' I said gently. 'Let's go and run you a bath.'

She hardly said a word as we traipsed wearily upstairs.

I put the plug in the bath and turned on the taps. Soon the bathroom was filled with steam.

'I'm going to make it all nice and bubbly for you,' I smiled, putting in a generous squirt of bubble bath and swirling the water around.

I could see Coco was staring in wonder at what I was doing.

'Are you OK, flower?' I asked her. 'Have you got a bath at home?'

She nodded.

'But not like your one,' she said. She dipped her hand in the water and wiggled it around. 'Your one is so warm.'

She got herself undressed and I helped her step into the bath. I could see the look of pure contentment on her face as she lay back in the bubbly water and closed her eyes.

'Do you know how to wash yourself?' I asked, handing her a flannel.

She nodded.

I chatted away to her as I folded up her clothes and got her a towel ready.

'Can I stay in a long time?' she asked.

'Of course,' I told her. 'You can have a lovely long soak until your skin goes all wrinkly like a prune.'

She let out a little giggle. It was nice to hear her laugh and I could see how much she was enjoying it.

'How do you get it like this?' she asked me.

'Get what?' I replied.

'How do you get the water warm?' she said, pointing to the taps.

'It just comes out that way,' I told her. 'The tap on the left is the hot tap and the one on the right is cold water.'

Coco looked amazed.

'Isn't it like that at home?'

She shook her head.

'Only cold comes out of our ones,' she sighed.

I was taking it all in, trying not to ask too many questions but at the same time, curious to find out more.

'Ooh, I bet a cold bath is a bit chilly,' I smiled. 'If the water's cold, how do you manage to wash yourself?'

'We do a magic wash in that,' she said, pointing to the sink.

'A magic wash?' I gasped. 'That sounds really special.'

'That's what Mummy calls it,' smiled Coco.

'Oh, I've never had a magic wash before,' I said. 'Can you tell me what you do?'

Coco explained how they got the flannel and put it under the tap and then gave themselves a wash.

'You have to do it really quick 'cos the water is freezing but then Mummy wraps us up like a sausage roll in a towel.'

'And does Mummy have a magic wash too?' I asked her. Coco nodded.

'When I see Mummy, I can tell her about the hot tap and maybe we can get one too,' she smiled.

I could see how much she was enjoying splashing about in the warm bath and it broke my heart to realise that she and her sister didn't have access to something as essential as hot water. I often came across children who lived in terrible conditions but what was different about Coco's situation was that their mum had tried to make a bad situation into a positive. Even though they were having to bathe in freezing cold water, by calling it a magic wash Zoe was trying to make it fun for them.

When Coco was dry and in her pyjamas, I tucked her up in bed. I could see her looking over sadly to the bottom bunk bed where Lola had slept the previous night.

'Sleep tight,' I told her. 'And remember, in the morning we're going to the hospital to see your sister.'

She lay back and nodded. A few seconds after her head hit the pillow, her eyes were already closed.

'Night night, Coco,' I whispered.

I went to see Amena, who was in her bedroom doing her homework again.

'How are you doing?' I asked her. 'I feel like I've hardly seen you.'

'You've been busy since the little girls came,' she replied.

'I certainly have,' I sighed. 'Hopefully Lola will be out of hospital soon and things will get a little calmer.'

I gave her a hug.

'I know it's early but I'm shattered, lovey, so I'm going to go to bed now,' I told her. 'Coco is fast asleep too.

64

I've locked up downstairs so are you OK to get yourself to bed?'

She nodded.

'No later than ten,' I told her. 'Remember it's a school night.'

'I know,' she sighed, rolling her eyes in the way that teen-agers like to do.

As I brushed my teeth, I worried that I'd have too much to think about and that my mind would be racing too much for me to sleep. But as soon as I lay down on my bed and closed my eyes, I nodded off.

The next thing I knew it was 7 a.m. and my alarm was going off next to me. Groggily, I hit the 'off' button. I looked down and realised that I'd been so tired, I'd fallen asleep on top of the covers.

I walked out onto the landing where thankfully every-thing was quiet. I peered into Coco's bedroom and I could see she was still curled up fast asleep. I gently pulled the door to and went to make sure Amena was up.

After a good night's sleep, I felt like a new woman. I whizzed through the house, getting all of my jobs done. By the time Amena had left for school, I'd made us both breakfast, put a wash on, emptied the dishwasher, done some emails and written up my recordings from the previous twenty-four hours, after the girls had arrived. It was normally something that I did at the end of each day and then emailed it to Becky at my agency, but she knew things were all up in the air with Lola in hospital.

I also called the hospital to see how Lola was doing.

'She's had a settled night,' the ward sister told me as I breathed a sigh of relief. 'She's a lot more alert this morning and she's even managed a little bit of breakfast.'

'That's brilliant,' I replied. 'I'm going to be coming up this morning with Lola's big sister so I'll talk to the doctor then.'

I had no idea of when Lola might be well enough to be discharged but at least things were moving in the right direction.

I was taking some clean washing upstairs when I heard loud sobbing coming from Coco's room.

She was sitting up in bed, crying hysterically.

'Lola's gone away,' she wept. 'Where is she?'

'Coco, it's OK,' I soothed. 'Remember that Lola was poorly so she went to the hospital so the doctors could give her medicine to make her better?'

Coco nodded as she started to wake up properly.

Poor little thing, I thought. With young children especially, it always tended to be the last thing at night when they were tired or the first thing in the morning when reality hit them. After being asleep, young children tend to forget what has happened. Then when they wake up in a strange room in a strange house, it can often trigger them and they become upset about where their mummy or daddy is.

'I bet Lola's going to be so pleased to see you,' I smiled. 'Shall we go downstairs and get some breakfast and then we can get dressed and go straight to the hospital?'

Coco nodded and the knowledge that she was going to see her sister thankfully seemed to console her.

An hour later, we were ready to leave.

In the car, Coco hardly said a word.

'Have you ever been to a hospital before?' I asked and she shook her head.

I described how Lola had her own bed in a ward with five other children.

6

'There's even a toy room at the end of it,' I told her.

'Can I play with them?' she asked me.

'I'm sure the nurses will let you,' I nodded. 'Although I'm not sure Lola's well enough to get out of bed yet.'

When we got to the hospital and parked, I tried to prepare her. I explained that Lola had a little tube taped to the back of her hand and that the tube led to some bags of fluid that were on a metal stand next to her bed.

'In those bags are the medicine that will make Lola better,' I added. 'And the tube means they go straight into her body and make her better much quicker than if she was swallowing it like you normally do.'

'Does it hurt Lola?' asked Coco.

'It might have hurt a tiny bit when the nurse first put the tube into her hand but it doesn't now,' I reassured her.

She was still very quiet as we walked through the doors of the hospital, and as we weaved our way past the busy A&E department and down the corridors, I felt Coco's little hand reach for mine. I gave it a reassuring squeeze.

'Here we are,' I said cheerily as I pressed the buzzer to the ward door.

A few minutes later, a nurse let us in.

'Lola's bed is just down here on the left,' I told Coco as we walked down the ward.

Today the curtains were open and Lola was sitting up in bed.

'Lola!' yelled Coco.

She still looked very frail and pale but her face broke out into a huge smile when she saw her big sister.

Coco instantly climbed onto the bed to give her a hug.

'Coco, be very careful of her wires,' I told her gently. 'You don't want to knock them out.'

'Ah, she'll be grand,' said Sorcha, who was back on duty. She put a plastic beaker of water and a straw on the table next to Lola's bed.

'Now is this your sister?' she asked Lola and she nodded. 'I could tell that as you've both got the same gorgeous golden hair,' Sorcha said. 'What lovely girls you are.'

She turned to Coco. 'Your little sister is much better today. But can you tell her that she needs to have a big drink for me?'

Coco nodded.

'Lola, the lady says you need to have a big drink,' she told Lola in her sternest voice, wagging her finger at her little sister.

Sorcha and I laughed.

'Good girl,' Sorcha smiled. 'I can tell who's the boss in your family.'

Coco clearly took her duties as a big sister very seriously. She picked up the beaker and carefully held it to Lola's mouth while she took a few sips from it.

'Are you feeling all right, Lola?' I asked her. 'Is your cough better?'

She nodded. She still looked very tired but thankfully she wasn't feverish any more.

When Lola had finished having a drink, Coco carefully put the cup back on the side then put her arm protectively around her sister. She looked down at the cannula in her hand.

'Is that your special medicine?' she asked, and Lola nodded.

'Poor Lo Lo,' she sighed, gently rubbing her sister's arm affectionately.

It was lovely to see them both cuddled up on the bed together and I could see how much comfort they got from each other.

Coco chatted away to her.

'Did you know Maggie's got a daughter? Her name is Louisa and she's a big girl. And she's got a baby called Edie and we played toys. Maggie's got toys in the kitchen and she's got a tap and warm water comes out of it so I had a bath and not a magic wash.'

I could see Lola was tired as she didn't say much but she listened contentedly as her sister talked away.

'Coco, guess what? I saw Mummy,' said Lola suddenly in a croaky voice.

My heart sank. This was what I had been worried about.

Coco's face fell and she sat up on the bed.

'How come?' she gasped.

'Mummy came to see me and gave me a cuddle,' said Lola.

Coco turned to me.

'But that's not fair,' she whispered, tears filling her eyes. 'I want to see Mummy too.'

'I know you do, flower,' I said sympathetically. 'And we're trying our hardest to make sure that you see her as soon as possible. Mummy came to see Lola as she knew that she was poorly in hospital and she was very worried about her.'

Coco nodded. I could see that she didn't want to make a fuss in front of her little sister but her eyes were brimming with tears.

'I promise that as soon as we get home, I will call Pamela and ask when you can see Mummy.'

Coco, bless her, didn't let her disappointment affect how she treated her sister and she snuggled back up with Lola on the bed. I could see Lola was getting very tired and her eyes were heavy.

Sorcha had also noticed.

'I think your sister could do with a rest now,' she said gently.

'Come on, lovey, I think it's time for us to go and let Lola have a sleep,' I told her.

Coco nodded and looked down at Lola nestled in her arms.

'Bye bye, Lo Lo,' she said, gently kissing her on the top of her head. 'Get better soon.'

I had a quick chat to Sorcha.

'I'll ring up later to see how she's doing,' I told her.

'Of course,' she smiled. 'I think she needs another restful day.

'But don't you worry, sweetie,' she said to Coco. 'Your little sister's doing a lot better.'

She nodded.

It had been one of the most stressful starts to a placement that I could remember in a long time. All I could hope was that things would be a lot calmer from now on.

SEVEN

Making Assumptions

On the way back from the hospital, I quickly called into the local supermarket to get some clothes for the girls. They'd come with the bare minimum and I wanted to get some more pyjamas for them both and a few things just to tide them over until we knew more about what was happening.

'Is there anything you like the look of?' I asked Coco as we walked up the aisles of the girls' section. 'What about some jumpers and leggings, or do you prefer jeans or skirts?'

Coco looked overwhelmed.

'Do you like these?' I said, holding up a pair of blue unicorn pyjamas.

'I like them all,' she nodded.

She watched me put them in the shopping trolley and her mouth gaped open.

'What, you can just buy them?' she asked.

'Yes, you and Lola need a few more things,' I nodded.

She seemed to be in a state of disbelief as I got her to choose herself and Lola a couple of jumpers each, some jeans and leggings and packs of knickers.

We were walking over to the food section through the toy department, when I saw a shelf of pink fluffy teddies.

'I know – shall we get Lola one of these?' I asked Coco. 'It might be nice for her to have a teddy that she can cuddle in hospital. Do you think she'd like that?'

Coco nodded eagerly.

'And if Lola has one, it seems only fair that you should have a matching one too,' I smiled, as I took two off the shelf and put them in the trolley.

'What, I can have my own one?' she gasped.

'Yes,' I nodded. 'I like to be fair and I think it would be nice for you to have something to cuddle too.'

I needed to quickly grab a few items from the food section. Again, Coco looked shocked as I put things in the trolley.

'Are you going to get all this?' she asked me.

'Yes,' I nodded. 'There's three of us in the house, and there will be four when Lola comes back, so we'll get through quite a lot of food.'

She looked even more confused when I got my bank card out to pay at the checkout.

'What's that?' she asked.

'It's my bank card,' I told her.

'But where's the money?' she asked in a panicked voice. 'Have you run out? It's OK, I can go and put the things back.'

'Don't worry, lovey,' I reassured her. 'We won't have to put anything back.'

Coco didn't look convinced and I could see that she was anxious.

'Do you sometimes have to put things back?' I asked and she nodded.

'Lots of times,' she said. 'When we went shopping a long time ago, Mummy didn't have enough pounds and we had to put things back. And one time Lola got sad 'cos she really liked the beans with sausages in the can but Mummy said she had to put it back. And I had to put the creamy milk back and now we've got the yucky powder one that me and Lola don't like.'

'Gosh, that must have been really disappointing,' I said. 'But don't worry, I've got enough money on my bank card to be able to pay for it.'

I explained that a bank was a place that looked after my money and when I wanted to spend it, I could use the card to pay for things.

Coco's face lit up.

'I know, I'll tell my mummy and she can get one of those special cards then we don't have to put things back or go to the church ever again.'

'What's the church?' I asked her.

'When Mummy hasn't got enough pounds, we go to the church and the lady gives us a box of things and we can take them home and we don't have to give her any money. You should go to one of them, Maggie.'

I listened, taking it all in. It was clear that things had been a real struggle for their mother.

All the way home in the car, I looked in the rear-view mirror to see Coco staring in wonder at her teddy and stroking its fleecy fur. It was just a small £5 thing but I could see how much it meant to her.

We pulled up outside my house and I was just walking up the front path with the bags of shopping when my mobile rang.

'Is it convenient to pop round now, Maggie?' asked a voice.

'Oh, hello, Pamela,' I said, fiddling with my keys in the lock. 'We've just got back from the hospital but we're home now so yes, any time is fine.'

She wanted to come and meet Coco and update me on things.

'Super,' she said. 'See you soon.'

When we'd got our shoes and coats off, I took Coco through to the kitchen and got her a biscuit and a beaker of orange squash.

'That was Pamela on the phone,' I told her. 'She's your new social worker and she's going to come round and say hello to you. Do you know what a social worker is?'

Sometimes we used these terms to children, who often didn't have a clue what we meant.

Coco shook her head.

'A social worker is someone who listens to children to find out what they need and who makes sure that they're OK and hopefully sorts everything out so that things are better for you and Lola.'

'And lets me see Mummy like Lola did?' she asked.

'Yes, she will organise for you to see your mummy and I will make sure that I ask her about that as I know how much you want to see her,' I replied.

Coco nodded.

I could see that she was tired after visiting Lola in the hospital so I let her have some TV time while I made us a sandwich. I knew Pamela could be arriving at any time but at least lunch would be ready.

It was another half an hour before there was a knock at the door.

'Come on in, Pamela,' I smiled.

'Coco,' I called. 'Pamela is here.'

Pamela swished through the front door in a long floral dress and the same waterfall cardigan.

I led her into the front room and turned off the TV.

'Hello,' she said in an overly loud, exaggerated baby voice. 'You must be Coco. I'm Pamela, your social worker. Maggie's been telling me what a brave girl you've been.'

Coco stared at her with a confused look on her face.

'I've explained to Coco that you're here to help her and Lola and make sure that they're OK,' I told her.

'That's right,' smiled Pamela in her sickly sweet voice. 'Is there anything you want to ask me?'

'When can I see my mummy please?' said Coco. 'Lola saw her and I want to see her too.'

'Well, I was just going to have a talk to you about that,' Pamela told her.

It was normal practice that a new social worker would want to spend some time with a child and get to know them.

'I'll go and make us all a drink while you two have a little chat,' I smiled.

I could see the panicked look on Coco's face as she realised that I was going to leave the room. She'd been polite to Pamela but I sensed that she hadn't exactly warmed to her.

'I'll only be next door in the kitchen,' I said. 'Pamela, would you like a cup of tea or would you prefer a coffee?'

'Ooh I'd love a coffee,' she replied. 'Do you have a cafetière?'

'I'm afraid not,' I shrugged. 'I've just got instant.'

'Oh, don't worry, I'll just have a glass of water,' replied Pamela.

I nodded. 'And I'll get you a juice, Coco.'

As I went off to the kitchen, I realised my feelings about Pamela were the same as Coco's.

When I went back in with their drinks, Pamela was talking away and Coco was staring at her with an unsure look on her face.

'There you go,' I smiled. 'I'll be in the kitchen if anyone needs me.'

I busied myself with some cleaning and ten minutes later, Pamela came into the room.

'I've put the TV back on for her,' she told me.

'So, Maggie, how are things from your perspective?' Pamela asked me as we sat down at the kitchen table. 'I know it must have been a strange thirty-six hours for you, but how's Coco been?'

'Considering everything that's happened and how scared and unstable she must be feeling, she's doing amazingly well,' I sighed.

'That's good to hear,' nodded Pamela. 'She's had a lot to cope with. And what are your first impressions of the girls?'

'They're not at all what I was expecting,' I told her.

'In what way?' she asked.

'Well, they have lovely manners – they say please and thank you,' I told her. 'They sit nicely at a table to eat and Coco can use a knife and fork. They know about personal hygiene. They brush their teeth and go to the toilet themselves.'

Many children who came into my care who had suffered neglect didn't have these basic skills. I'd hand them a toothbrush and they'd look very bemused because they didn't have a clue what to do with it. No one had ever shown them how to brush their teeth or cared if they did. Sadly, so many children didn't have the most basic of hygiene skills that we're taught when we're little. They didn't know how to wipe themselves after they'd been to the toilet, they didn't know to flush the loo or wash their hands. However, these were all skills that came naturally to Coco and Lola.

'It's clear to me there's been a fair amount of adult input in their lives,' I said. 'Put it this way, unlike a lot of children that I foster, I can tell that they've been nurtured and cared for.'

'Well, I wouldn't call being left every night while your mum goes out being cared for,' sighed Pamela.

'I agree that it's not good practice to leave young children home alone at night but I think we need to find out more about why that happened before I can make a proper judgement,' I said.

I hadn't even met Zoe yet.

'Well, I've spoken to Zoe and it was all of the usual excuses,' said Pamela wearily. 'Lack of childcare, no money, couldn't work or pay the bills and the rent.'

To me, they were all valid reasons why someone had struggled but Pamela wasn't being very empathetic to say the least.

'How did Mum's visit to the hospital go last night?' I asked. 'I bet Lola was very pleased to see her.'

'Well, she appeared to be,' sighed Pamela. 'And there were lots of tears from Zoe. Whether they were genuine or not remains to be seen.'

'Why wouldn't they be?' I asked. 'Her daughter was seriously ill in hospital; she must have been worried sick.'

'She gave that impression but, as you and I know, Maggie, some parents are very good at putting on an act, especially at the beginning of this process,' she shrugged. 'And she was probably crying because she knew that she was responsible for Lola being in hospital.'

'Zoe didn't give Lola pneumonia,' I replied, shocked that she'd said something so ridiculous.

'No, but living in a freezing cold, damp flat with no heating probably didn't do her daughter's health any good.'

It felt like Pamela was always looking for the negative.

'What's going to happen now?' I asked her, changing the subject.

'The police haven't charged Zoe yet but I think it's inevitable that they'll charge her with neglect,' said Pamela. 'In terms of Social Services, we'll probably start a parenting assessment, which no doubt is going to be a complete waste of time,' she sighed, rolling her eyes. 'And then we've got a problem because the little one could get adopted quite easily but people generally don't want seven-year-olds.'

I couldn't believe what I was hearing.

'Gosh, it's very soon to be thinking about adoption,' I replied.

'We have to think about that, Maggie, it's our job. We have to start planning for all of the options and I think it's very likely to happen in this case.'

'Why?' I asked.

Mum hadn't had a proper contact session with either girl and she hadn't even started a parenting assessment. Admittedly they were often hard for birth parents as they felt like they were being put under the microscope and scrutinised but they gave Social Services a good indication of what type of parent they were.

'Maggie, I've been doing this job for thirty years and I've seen it all before,' sighed Pamela. 'A mum who leaves her kids, especially one who's very sick, to go out at night, is not a fit mother. Do we really need an assessment to tell us that?'

'But from what you've said about Zoe, I don't get the impression that she was out partying,' I added. 'The girls seem to think that she was going out to work.'

'Where she was going and why is irrelevant,' Pamela replied. 'The facts speak for themselves. She's left young children alone at night in a freezing cold flat with no heating or electricity. Anything could have happened. She's very lucky she was arrested when she was, otherwise it could have been a very different story for Lola. She is clearly someone who shouldn't have sole responsibility for two young children.'

I didn't say anything, but I was appalled by the assumptions that Pamela was making. She was allowing herself to be jaded by past experiences and that's a dangerous thing for a social worker, or anyone, to do. It felt like she'd already made the decision about what was going to happen to the girls and there wasn't an ounce of positivity there. In fact, I'd never heard a social worker even considering adoption at their very first meeting with a child.

Over the years, occasionally I'd come across a social worker like Pamela before – normally they were close to retirement and weary of the job, thought they knew it all and weren't prepared to listen to anyone else's views. As soon as they were assigned a case, it was as if they'd already made their mind up which way it was going to go before talking to the children and everyone else involved.

I tried to put my feelings to the back of my mind for now as there were other things that Pamela and I needed to discuss.

'What's the latest news on contact?' I asked her. 'Lola unfortunately let slip this morning that she'd seen their mum and understandably Coco was very upset.'

'Yes, Coco did tell me that,' she replied. 'I explained to her that I'd managed to get a slot at a contact centre tomorrow morning.'

'That's great,' I sighed.

'Zoe has specifically asked if you could be there so she can meet you,' Pamela told me. 'Is that OK with you?'

'Absolutely,' I nodded.

As a foster carer, I often faced a lot of hostility from birth parents. I was seen as 'the enemy' and it was rare for them to want to meet me. They could be very resentful that I had their children and ultimately, even though it was Social Services who had made the decision, they saw me as the person who had taken their children away from them and there was a lot of blame and anger.

I'd been abused and threatened at contact sessions, confronted afterwards and even followed. On the occasions that that happened, I'd had to put a plan in place where I arrived much earlier to drop the children off and arrived later to pick them up after the birth parents had left. In those sorts of situations, I always had to remind myself that it was nothing personal. It was horrible and upsetting but I had to remember that they were angry at the system and not me.

I liked it when birth parents wanted to meet me and were prepared to work with me and Social Services. It made life so much easier for all of us.

Pamela took a final sip of her water and explained that she had to be going.

'Maggie, just to let you know that I'm going to pop up to the hospital this afternoon to see Lola so you don't have to go,' she told me.

'OK,' I said. 'I think I'll give the ward a ring anyway to check she's OK and put my own mind at rest. Is Zoe going to go and visit her again today too?'

'She did ask but I said we couldn't possibly organise that again so soon and it would have to be tomorrow,' said Pamela.

I wasn't sure why she'd said that as she was obviously going to the hospital herself anyway, but it was up to her to allow it or not as she had to be there during the visit.

'Right then,' she sighed, getting up. 'I will see you and Coco at contact tomorrow.'

'Yep,' I smiled.

After Pamela had gone, my head was spinning and I couldn't stop thinking about what she'd said and about all the assumptions that she'd made about Zoe. I was intrigued to meet Zoe myself and make up my own mind.

'That's such good news that you can see Mummy tomorrow,' I said to Coco as we tucked into our sandwiches.

She nodded.

'I wish it was this day,' she sighed sadly.

'I'm sure the time will go really quickly, flower,' I told her.

As I was clearing up the plates, my phone rang. It was my friend and fellow foster carer Vicky.

'Hi Maggie,' she said cheerfully. 'Just checking I'm still OK to bring the boys round this afternoon?'

My heart sank. I'd completely forgotten about that.

'Vicky, I've just had a new placement come in and my head's all over the place.'

I explained what had happened and how Lola was in hospital with pneumonia.

'Oh gosh, Maggie, I'm sorry,' she gasped. 'Poor little thing. Is she going to be all right?'

'I think so,' I said. 'She seems to be through the worst of it now.'

'Let's rearrange for another time,' Vicky told me. 'You've got a lot on your plate – the last thing you need is me and the boys coming round.'

But when I thought about it, I realised that Coco and I had nothing else planned for the rest of the day, and Pamela was going up to the hospital so I knew someone was with Lola.

'You know what, it's fine,' I said. 'I think we could both do with the distraction.'

'As long as you're sure?'

'Please come round,' I told her. 'I could do with a chat.'

For the past six months, Vicky had been fostering three brothers – six-year-old Grant, John, ten, and Robert, thirteen. They'd come from a family where their dad had been violent to their mum and both parents were alcoholics. They had some really challenging behaviour, especially the older two boys, and it had been a struggle for Vicky, who was a single carer like me. However, they were really starting to calm down. Grant, especially, had become very attached to Vicky and was very affectionate with her.

'My friend Vicky's going to come round later with her children,' I told Coco and she seemed intrigued to meet them.

It was after 4 p.m. when they arrived.

'I've come with snacks,' smiled Vicky, putting down some packets of biscuits and doughnuts.

'You didn't need to do that,' I told her.

'Oh, I did,' she said. 'You know how much my three eat – they never stop.'

'Hello, boys,' I said. 'This is Coco.'

Coco smiled shyly at them.

'Where's that other lass that was staying with you last time?' asked Robert gruffly.

He was a big lad for his age and he had the same bright ginger hair as his younger brothers.

'You mean Amena?' I said. 'She's at school at the moment, lovey. She'll be home late tonight as she's got drama.'

The boys had been to my house lots of times so they knew their way round. The older two ran straight out into the garden for a game of football and I got out some toys for Coco and Grant to play with. They were shy with each other at first and Grant was clinging onto Vicky.

'Why don't you go and play with Coco,' she encouraged him gently. 'She's got the castle out – look. That's your favourite.'

She picked Grant up off her knee and put him down on the floor.

'Go on,' she told him. 'I'll be right here having a coffee with Maggie.'

'OK,' he smiled before running off to sit with Coco.

'He's a cutie,' I smiled.

'He really is,' nodded Vicky. 'He's so affectionate and I've been getting some lovely cuddles.'

We chatted about the girls. As Vicky was a foster carer too, I knew I could confide in her about their background and she would keep it confidential.

'Who's their social worker?' she asked.

'A woman called Pamela Griggs,' I said. 'Have you come across her before?'

Vicky shook her head.

'No, I don't think I've ever worked with any Pams,' she replied.

'Oh no, she's not a Pam, she's a Pamela,' I told her. 'She was very quick to remind me of that.'

'Oh, she's one of those is she?' laughed Vicky, rolling her eyes.

It was good to have a bit of a chat with someone about it.

'Well, I've got some exciting news to tell you,' smiled Vicky. 'As you know, I've been through a lot with the boys and I'm thinking of taking them on full time.'

'That's great,' I said. 'Are you going for permanency?'

'I want more than that,' she replied. 'I'm thinking of going for a Special Guardianship Order.'

Special Guardianship meant that Vicky could make all of the important decisions about the children without their birth parents' agreement and she would have parental responsibility for them until they were all eighteen. It was financially viable as she would receive the same fee that she did for fostering them.

'Wow, that's a big commitment,' I told her.

She'd been fostering for over twenty years and had opened her home – and her heart – to multiple children over the years.

'I'm getting tired,' she sighed. 'I've reached a point where I'd like some stability rather than have different children coming and going all of the time.'

I understood what she meant. Occasionally I felt the same, but I'd started fostering with the aim of making a difference to as many children as possible and I still stuck by that.

I had taken on Louisa permanently all of those years ago but it was a very different situation. Louisa didn't ever want to be adopted. Even though her parents had died, in her mind they would always be her mum and dad and they could never be replaced. I wanted to give her that stability but as she was only one child, financially I still had to continue fostering others.

'It's a brave decision but I'm really excited for you,' I said, giving her a hug. 'I can see how attached the boys have got to you over these past few months.'

'And I've got attached to them,' she smiled. 'I know it sounds corny, Maggie, but sometimes it just feels right.'

'Well, you've got to do it then,' I grinned.

I was really happy for her and her plans for the future.

Even though Vicky's visit had been a lovely distraction, I couldn't stop thinking about some of the things that Pamela had said earlier that day and they were really niggling away at me.

I knew I needed to raise my concerns with Becky, my supervising social worker, both to get them off my mind and also so that there was a record of them.

'I'm just ringing to flag something with you,' I told her on the phone. 'I'm really concerned that adoption is being mentioned so soon in relation to the girls.'

'Who on earth has said that?' she asked.

'Pamela,' I replied. 'It's far too soon to be making sweeping judgements. I mean Coco hasn't even seen her mum yet, for goodness sake.'

'I agree,' sighed Becky. 'That does sound worrying.'

'And from what she was saying about Zoe, she was really struggling to make ends meet and was in a bad financial situation. It's really unfair of Pamela not to take that into account and just brand her as neglectful.'

It was terribly important for anyone who worked in Social Services, or was involved in the care system, to keep an open mind. First and foremost, Social Services should come from a position where they are working with parents and their children to help them stay together. If that isn't possible, then they could look at the alternatives. But some of the assumptions Pamela had made were unfair and dangerous and I knew if it continued, I was going to have to speak out.

EIGHT

First Impressions

Bang.

The noise was loud enough to wake me from my sleep. It was just after 6 a.m., so not horrendously early but still an hour before my usual alarm.

Maybe I'd imagined it, I thought, sitting up in bed. Until . . .

Bang.

There it was again. This time I knew it definitely wasn't my imagination.

I pulled on my dressing gown and wandered down the landing. The noise was coming from Coco's room.

'Coco?' I asked in a quiet voice so I didn't wake up Amena. 'Are you OK in there, lovey?'

I pushed open the bedroom door to find Coco balancing on a little chair pulling clothes out of the wardrobe. There were clothes all over the floor and some on the bed.

'Coco,' I gasped. 'What on earth are you doing?'

'I'm packing mine and Lola's stuff,' she said proudly. 'So I'm all ready to go home with Mummy.'

She had the bag open on the floor that Zoe had sent with the girls when they'd first come to me, and she'd managed to fold some knickers and pyjamas into a neat pile. My heart sank. This was my fault; I obviously hadn't explained the idea of contact to her in a clear enough way.

'Let me get you down from there before you fall,' I said, lifting her off the chair.

Then I got her to sit on the bed with me.

'Coco, you're going to see your mummy today and spend some time with her but I'm afraid you're not going to be able to go home just yet,' I told her gently.

She looked up at me, her green eyes filling with tears that eventually leaked out and spilled down her face.

'But why?' she sobbed. 'That lady said Mummy's finished talking to the police.'

'Pamela was right,' I nodded. 'The police have finished talking to Mummy for now, but Pamela also needs to talk to her as well and then they need to sort a few things out. And while that's happening, you and Lola are going to stay here with me at my house.'

'But I want to go home,' she said, her voice quivering.

'I know you do,' I sighed. 'And I know it's hard, but you're going to see Mummy today. You can spend time with her and play with some toys with her or read a book and have a cuddle but right now you can't go home with Mummy.'

'Please,' she begged.

'I'm afraid it's not my decision, sweetie,' I said.

I could see how upset she was and I felt like I was breaking her heart but I had to be clear and matter-of-fact about it with her so there was no more confusion.

'Come on,' I told her. 'Let's go downstairs and have some breakfast and then you'll need to get dressed because soon it will be time to go and see Mummy. OK?'

For the next few hours, I made sure I kept Coco as busy as possible to take her mind off things. She helped me get breakfast for Amena then we washed and dried the dishes.

The contact session was being held at a centre called Oak Lodge that I'd been to a few times before. It was a forty-five-minute drive from my house but it was all very new and modern and much brighter and cheerier than some of the run-down sixties' prefabs that were the other options in the area.

I was just putting some snacks and drinks in a bag in case Coco got hungry on the journey, when my mobile rang.

'Is that Mrs Hartley?' asked a voice.

'Yes, it's Ms Hartley,' I said.

It was the ward sister from Lola's ward.

'What's happened?' I asked anxiously. 'Is she OK?'

'Don't panic, she's absolutely fine,' she said. 'I'm ringing with good news. The doctor has just done her rounds and she's decided that Lola's well enough to be discharged today. She'll need to continue with some antibiotics but other than that, she's good to go.'

'Oh, that's fantastic,' I sighed. 'Thanks so much for letting me know.'

I explained that I had an urgent appointment that morning but that I would be there to collect her in the afternoon.

After I put the phone down to the hospital, I gave Pamela a quick call to let her know what was happening.

'That's great news,' she said. 'What a relief. I bet Coco was pleased.'

'Actually I haven't told her yet,' I replied. 'She's got so much on her mind with contact happening this morning and I was worried it would all be too overwhelming for her. I think I'll tell her about Lola this afternoon before we go and pick her up.'

'I'm happy to go with whatever you think is best, Maggie,' Pamela told me.

After I'd put the phone down, I realised we needed to get a move on so that we weren't late. I reminded Coco to go to the toilet as we had a long journey ahead of us.

'We're going to set off to see Mummy now,' I told her and she nodded.

'How do you know the way?' she asked me. 'Did my mummy tell you where our flat is?'

I took a deep breath and felt so guilty that I was about to drop another bombshell.

'When we go and see Mummy, it's not going to be at your flat,' I told her gently. 'It's going to be in a building that Social Services call a contact centre. It's a special place where children go so they can see their parents.'

Coco looked so disappointed.

'I'm sorry,' I sighed. 'I thought Pamela had explained that to you when she talked to you yesterday. I've been to this contact centre before and it's got lots of lovely toys and books,' I told her. 'And it's even got a garden with a climbing frame and a sandpit. Does that sound good?'

She nodded although I could see she was still upset.

I chatted away to her in the car but Coco didn't say much and I didn't push her. I couldn't tell if it was nerves or excitement about seeing her mum – perhaps a bit of both.

As I pulled into the car park, I was reminded of what a lovely building this centre was. It had been brand new the first time I'd dropped some children off at a session here a few years ago. It had everything you could think of, from a large, bright kitchen with a dining table, several highchairs, a dishwasher, oven and washing machine to a bathroom where parents could bathe their children. At the back of the house was a conservatory with doors that opened out onto a large garden where there was a swing, a slide, a climbing frame and a sandpit.

There were also three large contact rooms where parents could spend time with their children. They were all beautifully decorated with bright modern wallpaper and squishy sofas and lamps and coffee tables so they felt cosy. It was such a refreshing change from most contact centres with their grubby, worn-out furniture and broken toys.

'Are you coming in too?' Coco asked me and I nodded.

'I'll come and say hello to your mummy so she knows who I am and then I'll leave you to spend some time together,' I told her. 'Pamela will be there as well.'

Social workers generally wouldn't go to contact sessions; they were usually run by contact workers who would write up a report afterwards. However, it was Zoe's first session and understandably Pamela wanted to see how she and Coco interacted with each other.

To get into the centre, we had to go through a large security door. As I pressed the buzzer for someone to let us in, I could see Coco peering intently through the glass.

'Where is she?' she said, panicking. 'I can't see Mummy.'

'She might not be here yet, flower,' I told her.

A receptionist let us in and I was just signing in at the front desk and showing my ID when Coco suddenly let out an ear-piercing shriek.

'Mummy!' she yelled, running into one of the contact rooms.

I walked over and lingered in the doorway. Pamela was in there with a young woman who I assumed was Zoe. I remembered Pamela telling me she was in her mid-twenties but she looked like a little girl. She was small and skinny with long, fine blonde hair just like the girls. She had on tatty tracksuit bottoms that were way too big for her and a faded baggy sweatshirt that was holey and worn. She lifted Coco into her arms and buried her face in her daughter's hair.

'I love you, Coco,' she wept. 'I've missed you so, so much.'

Her hands were shaking and tears were streaming down her face onto Coco's head.

'Eurgh, you're making me all wet, Mummy,' she scolded.

When she looked up and saw Zoe's tears, she gently stroked her cheek.

'Don't cry, Mummy,' she said in a soft voice. 'There are lots of toys here for us to play with.'

'I know, sweetheart,' smiled Zoe, tenderly kissing the top of her head and putting her back down on the ground. 'I've just missed you and Lola so much.'

I was still hovering in the doorway, watching it all unfold.

'Zoe, this is Maggie,' said Pamela, turning towards me.

'Hi, Zoe,' I smiled, walking into the room.

'Hello,' she replied.

Her face was pale and her cheekbones were sunken and there were dark black shadows under her green eyes. She looked as if she hadn't slept in days.

Coco had her arms around Zoe's waist and she was like a limpet, not wanting to let her mum go.

Zoe turned to her.

'You stay with Pamela for a minute, sweetheart, while I go and have a little chat with Maggie,' she told her. 'I promise I'll be back soon.'

'I know, let's look at these lovely toys,' said Pamela, trying her best to distract Coco.

Zoe and I walked out into the reception area where there was a sofa. She didn't make eye contact with me as she began to talk.

'I hope you don't mind but I wanted to meet the person who was looking after my girls,' she said. 'I just wanted to say thank you and I'm so, so sorry about all of this.'

'It's not a problem,' I told her. 'I'm happy to meet you; I'd be exactly the same if I was in your shoes. You've got two absolutely gorgeous girls.'

'I know,' she said, her voice wobbling with emotion. 'I still can't believe this is happening.'

I could see her hand was shaking as she lifted it to her face to wipe away her tears.

'I want you to know that I'm a good mum and I love my kids with all my heart. They're my world and I would never, ever hurt them. I know I've let them down but I'm going to sort this mess out and get them back as soon as I can. I miss them so much. I'd just got myself into a bad situation with money and I couldn't see a way out.'

'It's OK,' I told her. 'You don't have to justify yourself to me.'

'Thank you,' she nodded.

'How have they both been?' she asked, her face crumpled with worry. 'Are they eating and sleeping OK? They looked so scared that night they got taken away from me.'

'They're doing really well considering everything they've been through,' I told her. 'Obviously Lola's only had one night at my house before she went to hospital.'

'I'm so ashamed,' sighed Zoe. 'I didn't realise she was so ill. I'll never ever forgive myself for what happened. Thank you for taking her to the hospital.'

'It's OK,' I told her. 'We all make mistakes and little ones can deteriorate so quickly. The main thing is she's going to be OK.

'You must have been worried too,' I added.

'Oh, I've been worried sick,' Zoe sighed, wringing her hands. I noticed her fingers were all bloodied from where she'd peeled the skin off from around each nail.

'I don't think I've slept since they were taken into care,' she sighed. 'I don't think I can until I get them back.'

She looked like a woman in complete and utter distress, but the love she had for her girls was palpable. However, I also knew that although my instincts were telling me that Zoe was genuine, it was still very early days. 'The other reason I wanted to meet you, Maggie, was that there are some things I wanted you to know about my girls,' she said. 'Lola's got a special blanket that she loves which she calls blankie. I put it in the bottom of the bag I sent but you might not have seen it as it looks like an old rag. For some reason, she likes to wrap it around her fingers and stroke her nose with it. I know it sounds funny but it really soothes her to sleep.

'And Coco loves stories,' she continued. 'Not books but made-up stories. The crazier, the better,' she smiled. 'She especially likes stories where she does magical things like flying or jumping on the moon, then she often dreams about them.

'She's such an imaginative little thing,' she said. 'Sometimes she has bad dreams too. It's scary, she wakes up screaming. But I stroke her hair, which seems to calm her and eventually she'll drift back off.'

I nodded, trying to take it all in.

'I wanted to tell you all of these things,' she said. 'I've been laying there night after night worrying about the girls and wondering if they're managing to settle.'

'Thank you,' I smiled. 'I really appreciate that.'

'Oh, and Lola's scared of having her hair washed and she doesn't like water going over her face. Her favourite colour is purple and Coco likes yellow.'

Zoe was telling me all of this information because she wanted to and I could see she wanted her children to be OK.

'Are they in the same bedroom?' she asked. 'They're used to sleeping together.'

'Yes,' I told her. 'Don't worry, they are.'

I looked at the clock on the wall.

'It's been great chatting to you but I don't want you to waste any more time talking to me when there's a little girl in there desperate to see her mummy.'

'Thank you,' smiled Zoe. 'It means so much to me that the girls are in safe hands.'

I watched her go back into the contact room and close the door. The session was an hour-long and it wasn't enough time to go anywhere so I decided to sit in my car and catch up on some paperwork.

I kept one eye on the clock and, when the hour was up, I headed back inside. I wasn't looking forward to this part as I sensed Coco was going to be upset about having to leave her mum again.

When I got inside, the door of the contact room was open.

'Oh look, Maggie's here now,' I heard Pamela say. 'Time to say bye to Mummy.'

I walked into the room to see Coco sitting on Zoe's lap with her hands draped around her neck.

'Can we go home now, Mummy?' she asked her. 'I want to come back with you.'

I could see Zoe didn't know what to say to her.

'Coco, remember what we talked about earlier?" I told her gently. 'Remember, Mummy needs to do some more talking with Pamela so you are going to stay with me.'

'Yes, you need to go back with Maggie,' added Pamela. 'Because you've got somewhere very important to go this afternoon. Haven't you, Maggie?'

Coco looked at me and I nodded.

'The doctors have said that Lola is well enough to be discharged from the hospital so you and Maggie need to go and pick her up,' Pamela added.

Coco grinned.

'Oh, that's wonderful,' gasped Zoe.

But the relief on her face quickly turned to devastation as Zoe realised that she wouldn't be the one collecting her daughter from the hospital and bringing her home. Her lip started to tremble and I could see that she was struggling to hold back the tears.

'That's good, Mummy, isn't it?' said Coco. 'Lola's all better now.'

'It's brilliant,' smiled Zoe, desperately wiping her face and trying to hide her tears from her eldest daughter.

'Coco, it's time to say goodbye to Mummy now,' Pamela said.

Coco curled up on Zoe's lap and put her arms around her waist. Zoe closed her eyes and kissed the top of her head.

'I love you, Coco,' she told her. 'I'll see you and Lola very soon. Give Lola a kiss from me.'

Coco nodded.

I could see Zoe was putting on a brave face in front of Coco but I knew as soon as we left, she was probably going to crumble.

'Come on then, let's go and get your sister,' I said as cheerfully as I could.

It was important for the children's sake to try to keep goodbyes quick and upbeat. Contact was emotionally draining enough for them without everyone crying and struggling leave.

As we walked out of the room, Coco stopped, turned around and gave Zoe one last wave. It pulled at my heartstrings to see the look of pure sadness on her little face and I reached for her hand and gave it a gentle squeeze.

Coco was quiet as we walked across the car park but as soon as I shut the car door, she burst into tears.

'Hey,' I soothed from the front seat. 'It's OK. I know you're sad not to be going home with Mummy but you'll see her again soon.'

We had to go home first before we headed to the hospital. We needed to have some lunch and also collect some clothes for Lola to wear as she only had pyjamas at the hospital.

I could see how exhausted and drained Coco was after the heightened emotion of contact so I let her eat her sandwich in front of the TV. She just needed to switch off and zone out for half an hour.

I felt like I needed to do the same and I was making myself a cup of tea when Pamela called.

'So what did you think of Zoe?' she asked me. 'Did you notice how skeletal and pale she was? I've got a sneaking suspicion there may be drugs involved.'

I was surprised that she'd come to that conclusion.

'I certainly didn't get that impression at all,' I told her. 'She was very thin and looked exhausted but I think it's the worry and the fact that she's not sleeping.'

Zoe didn't have that ravaged, wrung-out look that drug addicts often had. Yes, she was pale but she wasn't spotty and I hadn't noticed any scabs or sores on parts of her body.

'Oh, I did,' sighed Pamela. 'I watched her when she was talking to you and she was shaking a lot and wringing her hands almost like she needed her next fix.'

'I actually thought that was anxiety and she was very distressed,' I responded.

I didn't agree with any of Pamela's observations. Zoe struck me as someone at their lowest. She was at absolute rock bottom because her kids had been taken away. She didn't know where to turn or what to do next.

To me, she seemed totally genuine. But I knew it was early days and I had to force myself to take a step back. Years of fostering had taught me that first impressions could often be very wrong. I'd worked with parents who seemed delightful at first and it had looked as if there had been a terrible mistake taking their children into care. But as the weeks had gone by, it was hard for them to keep the façade up and eventually their mask had slipped.

'The truth will out itself eventually, Maggie,' sighed Pamela.

Yes, it will, I thought. And it couldn't come soon enough.

NINE

Homecoming

We walked through the hospital doors, Coco skipping along beside me.

'Will Lola be able to walk to the car?' she asked me. 'Can she eat food?'

'I think so,' I told her. 'We'll have to see what the doctors say.'

I hadn't actually seen her for over twenty-four hours but I was pleased that she was being discharged. It was such a relief to know she was going to be OK.

When we got to the ward, Lola was sitting up in bed. She was still very pale but the cannula was out of her arm and she looked so much better.

'Are you feeling OK, flower?' I asked her and she nodded.

Coco climbed straight onto the bed next to her.

'Guess what, Lola? I saw Mummy today. I went to this big building and there were loads of toys and Maggie said there was a climbing frame in the garden but I didn't go on it.'

Now it was Lola's turn to feel aggrieved.

'Next time, you can both see Mummy together,' I reassured her.

'Will there be toys?' she asked me.

'Yes,' I nodded. 'It will be at the same contact centre where Coco went and there are lots of toys and books there.'

'Can we go soon?' added Coco.

'Pamela's going to do her best to set something up in the next few days,' I told her.

Sorcha the nurse came over to us.

'Ah, Lola, I hear you're going home today,' she smiled. 'That's great news.'

Coco's face crumpled.

'That's not fair!' she gasped. 'How come Lola can go home and I can't?'

Sorcha gave me an apologetic look.

'No, lovey,' I explained. 'By "home", she means my home and not your flat. Lola is coming back to my house with us.'

'Is Mummy coming too?' asked Lola.

I could see how confusing it must be for them both, especially for Lola who had spent more time at hospital than at my house.

'No, Lola,' Coco told her. 'Mummy is at our flat and Maggie says she has to talk to that lady and then we can go home.'

'That's right,' I nodded. 'Mummy needs to talk to Pamela, your social worker. Remember the lady who came to see you yesterday?'

Lola nodded.

'They still need to sort a few things out and Pamela needs to check that you and Coco are safe and happy and that Mummy is too, so for now, you're both going to be sleeping at my house.'

Lola nodded although I wasn't sure if she was really taking any of it in. She was only three and so much had happened to her over the past few days.

Sorcha came back in, clutching a paper bag.

'The doctor wants Lola to take a course of these,' she said, handing me the package of antibiotics. 'You also need to make sure that she keeps well hydrated. Any problems or if you're worried about anything at all, take her straight to the GP or give us a call.'

'Thank you,' I told her.

'I'm sorry about before,' she told me in a low voice. 'I didn't mean to confuse the girls.'

'It's OK,' I said. 'They're both struggling to work things out in their own heads. It's not your fault.'

I made a mental note to try not to refer to my house as 'home' any more as it was too confusing for them.

'Right then, shall we get you dressed, Lola, and then get you back to my house?'

'Maggie, we forgot to give Lola her surprise,' said Coco suddenly.

'Oh yes,' I replied. 'Do you want to get it out for her?'

Coco quickly unzipped the bag and handed Lola the little pink teddy. Her face lit up.

'I got one too,' Coco told her. 'Maggie just bought them with a special card, she didn't even need any pounds.'

Lola looked absolutely ecstatic with her little bear.

'Come on then, let's get you up and dressed,' I told her.

'Maggie got you some clothes from the shop,' Coco told her. 'And I got some too. They're brand new.'

I could see Lola was as amazed by this as Coco had been.

I quickly helped her into some leggings and a jumper and put some socks on her and the worn old trainers she'd arrived in, which I could see were way too tight and had holes in the sole. I reminded myself to take the girls to the shoe shop later in the week.

Lola was still very weak so the ward nurse got a porter to bring us a wheelchair so I could push her out to the car. Coco ran along next to her and Lola giggled. It was nice to see her smile even though she still seemed so frail.

Fifteen minutes later, we finally pulled up at my house.

'Do you remember being here?' I asked Lola.

She'd arrived late at night in the dark and the next day when I'd taken her to the hospital she'd been very poorly. She shook her head.

'Don't worry, Lola, I'll show you around,' Coco told her.

She took her hand and pulled her into all of the rooms downstairs. Then they went upstairs to their bedroom where I could hear Coco chatting away.

'Look, we've got real beds with legs,' she told Lola. 'That's your one and this is my one. And guess what? Maggie's got a tap and hot water comes out of it and I had a bath with bubbles in it, not a magic wash.'

'Me have one too?' asked Lola, and Coco nodded.

She also told her about Amena and Louisa and Edie and my big cupboard in the kitchen that was full of toys.

While Lola had the full guided tour, I quickly messaged Becky and Pamela to let them know that Lola was back from the hospital. I hoped Pamela would pass the message on to Zoe so it would put her mind at rest.

Lola didn't eat much tea and by 6 p.m. I could see she was

absolutely exhausted. She was coughing occasionally and I could see her little body was still recovering so I put her to bed.

'You're going to see Louisa and Edie again tomorrow,' I told Coco as I got her ready for bed and her face lit up.

It was unfortunate timing with Lola just being discharged, but the following day, a Looked After Child (LAC) review was being held at Social Services. This was normally organised within the first couple of weeks of a child coming into the care system. It was a chance for everyone involved in the child's care to get together, update each other and decide how things were going to proceed moving forwards. Zoe would have been invited to attend and Pamela would be there, as well as my supervising social worker Becky. There would normally be someone from the child's school there and in this case, I imagined someone from the police would be attending. The meeting would be chaired by someone called an Independent Reviewing Officer (IRO). All local authorities had a duty to appoint an IRO to every child in their care and it would normally be someone who worked for Social Services but wasn't directly involved in the case. The IRO's role was to make sure that the children's wishes and best interests were at the heart of every decision.

Luckily Louisa had a day off the following day and she had offered to come to my house with Edie to look after the girls. Thankfully Coco seemed happy with that and I hoped Lola would be too.

After I'd got both girls to bed, I sat at my computer and typed up my recordings about the day so I could email them to my agency. Three days in and I didn't feel any clearer about what was likely to happen going forwards. Hopefully the LAC review would give everyone a bit of clarity. At least Lola was out of hospital and both girls were under my roof now and I could start to get to know them and get them into a routine. Even though their whole world had fallen apart, children felt a lot of safety and security from routine and familiarity, and I hope that would be the case with the girls. I knew it was early days but I hadn't seen any signs of challenging or worrying behaviours. They seemed, on the face of it, like lovely girls and hopefully the following day a lot of my questions would finally be answered.

We had the quiet, uneventful night that we all desperately needed and everyone slept well. In the morning, both girls seemed happy to be staying with Louisa and Edie while I went to the meeting, which was being held at the large Social Services building in town. I always liked to try to be early so I could have a little catch up with Becky before the meeting started. Pamela was already there too, bustling around and she introduced me to the IRO, a woman called Heidi.

'She seems very young to me,' muttered Pamela in my ear. 'She doesn't look old enough to be a social worker, never mind an IRO.'

'She seems very friendly,' I shrugged.

IROs were always qualified social workers with at least five years' experience.

'I'm so sorry I haven't managed to meet the girls yet,' Heidi told me. 'I know Lola's only just come out of hospital.'

It was common practice to meet with the children before every review meeting but Heidi explained that she'd only been appointed the previous day.

'But if it's OK with you, I'll pop round early next week to have a chat to them both,' she added.

I was also about to ask if Zoe was intending to come to the review when the meeting room door swung open. Zoe stood there looking incredibly awkward and uncomfortable.

'Sorry,' she said, her head firmly looking down at the floor. 'I got a bit lost.'

She was wearing the same faded, worn tracksuit that she'd had on at contact the previous day. Her eyes were all puffy and swollen as if she'd been crying and she was clutching a tatty tissue in her hand. I could tell she didn't know where to put herself.

'There's a spare seat here,' I said, waving over to her.

'Thank you,' she nodded before weaving her way over to the side of the table where Becky and I were sitting.

My heart went out to Zoe. Whatever the circumstances that resulted in your children being taken into care, it must feel intimidating and overwhelming to walk into a room of child-protection professionals who were all there to talk about you and your children.

The child's birth parents were always invited to attend the reviews although many chose not to come. The child could come too if they were over sixteen.

'Right then,' smiled Heidi. 'Let's get started.'

She quickly outlined the circumstances in which the girls had come into the care system by reading out the report written by the duty social worker. She explained how the police had been called to a corner shop where Zoe had been accused of shoplifting.

'From the items that she'd stolen and her reaction to being told she was going to be questioned at the police station, the officers attending the scene soon realised there was more to this than met the eye initially. Zoe eventually admitted to them that she had two daughters who were at home alone. She agreed to co-operate with the police and they went to the flat, where they were met by Arti Kwatra, a social worker from Social Services.'

As she described the conditions the girls were found in, Zoe began to cry.

'Arti's report details that the flat was pitch black, freezing cold and damp. There was no electricity or heating, it was very sparsely furnished and there was mould on the walls. Both girls were huddled on the living-room floor, lying on top of sofa cushions to make a makeshift bed. There were no beds in the property. They were both scared and crying and told the social worker that "Mummy had gone out and left them". Arti also noted that Lola, the younger of the two girls, had a bad cough.'

Zoe let out a loud whimper. Even though they were the facts, it was hard to see someone in so much pain and I reached over and patted her hand.

'Arti states that the girls became hysterical when the police left with Zoe,' continued Heidi. 'They were crying and the eldest girl, Coco, was screaming, "Please don't take Mummy away". It took over an hour to calm them both down.'

Zoe shook her head. I could see how hard it was for her to hear all of this and she sat there with a look of utter despair on her face.

'I know what you're all thinking but I swear to you, I'm not a bad mother,' she wept. 'I love my girls.'

With that, she stood up, pushed the chair back from the table and ran out of the meeting room.

TEN

Difficult Conversations

Silence descended over the meeting room and everyone stared at the door that Zoe had just walked out of, unsure of what to say.

'Right then,' sighed Pamela. 'Where were we, Heidi?'

I couldn't believe that she was happy to carry on with the meeting as if nothing had happened.

'Excuse me for a minute,' I said, standing up and pushing back my chair. 'I'm going to check that Zoe's OK.'

It wasn't really my job to do this as my focus was supposed to be on the children, but I couldn't sit there knowing a young woman was just outside in deep distress.

I pushed open the door and walked out into the corridor. Zoe was sitting on the floor, her head in her hands, sobbing.

I crouched down next to her and put my arm on her shoulder.

'That must have been really hard for you to hear,' I said gently.

She nodded.

'I feel so guilty knowing the girls were so upset and I had caused that,' she snivelled. 'That Heidi woman called me before the meeting and said it might be upsetting for me but I didn't think it would be this bad.'

I couldn't imagine how she was feeling.

'I know this is really difficult but the best thing for you to do is to go back in there,' I told her. 'Everyone knows that it's taken a lot of courage for you to come here today and it shows the social worker and the IRO that Coco and Lola are your priority and you're prepared to work with them.'

If she didn't come back, people would be making decisions about her children without Zoe being able to say what she thought. While it was really hard for her, she needed to be in there to show her commitment to Coco and Lola.

'I don't think I can do it,' she sobbed. 'It will break my heart to hear any more.'

'It's up to you,' I told her. 'I've got to go back in now but you know where we are.'

I hoped that she would find the strength to come back.

Everyone turned to look as I pushed open the meeting room door.

'Sorry,' I said, going to sit back down.

'All OK?' whispered Becky and I nodded.

Heidi continued going through her notes, talking about when the girls had come to me and how Lola had been taken to hospital and treated for pneumonia.

Suddenly the door creaked open and Zoe appeared. With her head down, she scuttled back over to the seat next to me.

'Sorry,' she sniffed, not making eye contact with anyone. 'I needed the loo.'

I gave her a supportive smile.

'It's like musical chairs in here,' huffed Pamela.

Heidi picked up where she had left off and introduced us all to Coco's Year 2 teacher, Mrs Evans. She didn't look much older than Louisa, and had shiny blonde hair and was wearing a floral skirt and pink jumper. She looked smiley and kind, the epitome of what you'd imagine a primary school teacher to look like.

'Does Coco attend school regularly?' Heidi asked her.

'Her attendance has generally been good and she's pretty much there on time,' Mrs Evans nodded.

'Pretty much?' asked Pamela, peering over her glasses. 'What do you mean by that?'

'Oh, well, just that she's been late the odd morning,' added Mrs Evans, looking a bit flustered.

'Have you had any involvement with Mum?' Heidi continued.

'She comes to all of the parents' evenings and she's there every day to pick her up,' Mrs Evans replied.

Zoe looked over and gave her a weak smile.

'Mrs Evans, do you have any concerns about Coco?' asked Pamela. 'Have you noticed anything worrying in her behaviour or appearance, for example? Any bruising or marks on her?'

'Oh gosh, no, nothing like that at all,' Mrs Evans gasped. 'She's a really well-behaved little girl. And I've never seen anything beyond the usual scrape or scuffed knees from falling over in the playground.'

Then she paused. 'There's only thing that I have noticed and I feel very uncomfortable saying this . . .'

'Please go on,' encouraged Pamela.

111

'Her uniform has been a bit tatty at times. Don't get me wrong, it's not dirty. It just looks old. You know, polo shirts with holes in them, frayed skirts, everything's always too small and very worn and faded.'

Zoe looked mortified and stared down at the table.

'Did you ever say anything to Coco?' asked Heidi.

'Oh gosh no,' Mrs Evans replied. 'I'd never do that. I wouldn't want to make her feel embarrassed or ashamed. From time to time, I'd give Coco some uniform to take home. I wouldn't make a big deal of it; I'd put it in her bag over the course of the school year as and when I could see that she needed it.'

Mrs Evans explained that she would buy polo shirts, jumpers, trousers and skirts when she saw them on offer in the supermarket and give them to the pupils that she could see needed them.

'That's very kind of you,' smiled Heidi.

'Sadly it's just the way of the world these days,' she shrugged. 'I can see some parents are really struggling.

'I can tell Coco really loves school,' she added. 'She's always commenting on how lovely and warm it is in the classroom and I often see her draped over the radiator at break time. I get the feeling that perhaps unlike home, she knows it's a place where she'll always get a hot meal and feel warm.'

Pamela had her head down and was busy taking notes.

'Anything else that you've noticed about Coco that you think might be relevant?' she asked.

'The only other thing I should mention is that recently I've noticed there are times when Coco's very tired. In fact she's fallen asleep on a couple of occasions in class. I did keep her behind one day and asked her if she was OK,' said Mrs Evans. 'I said she seemed very tired and I asked her if she was feeling unwell.'

'And what did Coco say?' asked Pamela.

'Well, she very matter-of-factly told me that sometimes she found it hard to sleep because she didn't have a bed at home.'

'Did she say what she did sleep on?' asked Heidi.

'She said she and her little sister shared the cushions from the sofa that they put on the floor. She said her mummy slept on the floor but that she was saving up to buy them all a bed.'

By now, Zoe was slumped forward on the table with her head in her hands. It must have been so hard and painful for her to have the reality of her life laid wide open to everyone. It tallied up with what Coco had told me about their flat but it was still heartbreaking to hear.

'Were you surprised when Coco told you that she didn't have a bed?' asked Pamela.

'I was,' Mrs Evans nodded. 'I felt desperately sad that her and her sister didn't have something as basic as a bed. Something that I think most of us perhaps take for granted.'

'I'm sorry,' Mrs Evans said, turning to Zoe.

Zoe shook her head and burst into tears.

'I know I sound like a terrible mother who makes her children sleep on the floor,' she sobbed. 'I desperately wanted them to have beds but I just didn't have the money. I tried my best, I really did.'

Becky rummaged in her handbag and leant across the table to give Zoe a tissue.

'I'm sorry, Zoe, I can see this is really traumatic for you but it's really important for us all to build up a full picture of the girls' home life,' Heidi told her.

'I understand,' she said in a quiet voice.

Then it was my turn to speak. Heidi asked me how I'd found the girls so far.

'They've got very good manners,' I smiled. 'They come across as if they've had lots of nurturing. They're really lovely girls.'

'Any issues with their behaviour?' asked Pamela.

'Unlike many of the children that come to me, no,' I told her. 'So far, they've behaved beautifully. They understand boundaries and bedtimes and personal hygiene.'

'Do they ask about their mummy?' said Heidi.

'All the time,' I nodded. 'Ever since they arrived at my house, they've been constantly asking when they are going to see Zoe, and Coco was so pleased to see her at contact yesterday. All their distress has been about missing their mummy.'

There was something else that I wanted to add.

'I also wanted to say well done to Zoe for coming back into this meeting. I think we forget because we do these types of reviews all the time but it must be really hard for birth parents to sit here and listen to people picking apart their parenting. I feel that the fact that she's here today really shows her commitment to Coco and Lola.'

Heidi nodded in agreement at my words but Pamela had a face like thunder.

'Thank you,' Zoe whispered to me and I gave her a smile.

Then it was Pamela's turn to share her observations and she didn't hold back.

'I've seen Zoe three or four times now, and no matter how many assurances she keeps giving us about how much she cares for her children and how deeply she misses them, I find it very difficult to get past the fact that she has admitted to leaving them at home alone on a dark, cold night while also knowing that one of them was seriously ill.

'She's also admitted that it wasn't a one-off occurrence. From everything else we've been hearing today, she's also clearly struggled to meet the most basic of needs for her daughters. To me, Zoe isn't someone who has her children's best interests at heart.'

'But I told you, I was going to work,' gasped Zoe. 'I'm a single parent and I was struggling. If I didn't work then I couldn't pay the rent and I couldn't feed my girls. It seemed like the only way at the time. I swear I never wanted to leave them.'

Zoe looked stunned and I was shocked by the brutality of Pamela's words. There were ways of delivering information and if a parent was there, like Zoe was, you had to be mindful of how you said things.

Heidi was also clearly surprised, and she quickly tried to move the conversation on.

'Thank you, Pamela, for your contribution – I think we get the gist,' she said. 'Can you tell me what contact has been organised for the children?'

'Well, it's been very difficult to find a slot. Oak Lodge is always full and it's proving tricky to find space.'

'There are many different places children can see their parents and it doesn't necessarily have to always be at the same centre,' Heidi told her. 'I expect Mum to be having contact at least three times a week and we must stick to that,' she added firmly.

115

'That's easier said than done,' huffed Pamela, clearly not very happy that she'd been pulled up by Heidi.

'Shall we discuss this outside of the meeting, Pam?' Heidi suggested.

'Actually, it's Pamela,' she snapped.

One thing I had noticed was that there was no one from the police at the meeting and I asked Heidi about it.

'We did ask the police if they were able to attend today but unfortunately PC Davidson and PC Hunt, who attended the flat the night the girls were taken into care, were unavailable today,' Heidi told us. 'They did send us an update though.'

She looked down at her notes.

'They're still awaiting a decision from the Crown Prosecution Service but they think it's likely that Zoe will be charged with neglect.'

Zoe let out a gasp.

'They can't!' she shouted. 'It's not fair, they can't do this! What's going to happen to me?'

She was becoming hysterical.

I reached across and patted her hand to try to calm her down.

'Zoe, the police will get back to you first and let you know what's happening,' Heidi told her gently. 'I know this is hard for you to hear and frightening, but it's important for you to be prepared for the fact that you might face charges. And if that does happen, you'll have your chance in court to put your side of the story across.'

Zoe looked terrified.

An Emergency Protection Order generally only lasts seventy-two hours before Social Services have to go back to the courts and apply for what's known as an Interim

Care Order. However, Heidi informed us all that Zoe had agreed to a Section 20, where a birth parent agrees to let their children stay in the care system voluntarily. Again, that was a really positive thing for her to do as it demonstrated she was willing to work with Social Services. This was something that Pamela should have updated me on but I hadn't been informed.

Then it was up to Heidi to decide how things were going to progress going forwards.

'One thing I do think we're all agreed on is that Coco should start back at school next week,' she said. 'Maggie, I will leave that in your capable hands.'

'Absolutely,' I nodded. 'I'll have a chat to Mrs Evans after this meeting.'

'Obviously, Lola is still recovering from pneumonia but when she's feeling better, we should also look into the possibility of her attending pre-school,' Heidi added.

She turned to address Zoe.

'I feel the best way forwards from here is to start a twelve-week parenting assessment with you,' she said. 'Pamela, can you tell us when the assessment needs to start?'

'Oh, I was going to wait until we knew the outcome of the police investigation,' Pamela replied. 'I mean there's no point starting an assessment if she's going to get a custodial sentence is there?'

Zoe looked confused.

'What's a custodial sentence?' she asked.

'If you go to prison, dear,' Pamela told her bluntly.

Zoe's face crumpled and she started to cry.

'Am I likely to?' she asked and Pamela shrugged.

'Child cruelty can carry up to a maximum of ten years,' she told her.

Obviously that was only in extreme cases but I could see that understandably it had shaken Zoe to the core.

'I can't go to prison,' she wept. 'What about my girls? I was trying my best. The only way I could work was by leaving them.'

Even if she did get a custodial sentence, she could still come out and request an assessment on her release. It didn't automatically mean she would never get the girls back.

'We'll start the parenting assessment then we'll reassess when we know where we are with the criminal proceedings,' nodded Heidi. 'And the court will take into account any mitigating circumstances, such as your financial situation at the time.'

Zoe still looked absolutely stunned.

'Have you got any questions that you'd like to ask us, Zoe?' Heidi said.

'Will my girls stay with Maggie?' she said.

'I'm afraid we can't guarantee that,' Pamela told her.

'I'm more than happy to look after the girls until we know more about what's happening,' I told her.

'Thank you,' Heidi told me. 'So the next review will be in three months when hopefully we will have more clarity about what is going on.'

As the review meeting came to a close, everyone started to pack their things away but Zoe just sat there with her head in her hands. I really felt for her as it must have been so emotionally draining for her and she looked completely overwhelmed.

'Zoe, can I have a quick word with you to arrange the next contact session?' Pamela asked her. 'I also need some signatures on some papers.'

Heidi also needed to talk to her to check that she understood what had been said.

'Are you OK?' I asked Zoe, putting my hand on her shoulder.

'Not really,' she shrugged. 'I'm facing the fact that not only have I lost my girls but that now I could be locked up for years too.'

She looked terrified, and totally and utterly broken.

ELEVEN

Bombshells

There was nothing I could say to Zoe that would make things any better or take away her fears.

'What Pamela said to you in the meeting was the very worst-case scenario,' I told her. 'It might not happen like that.'

'But what if it does? I might have to go to prison for a long time and I probably deserve it.'

'Why don't you go and have a chat to Heidi?' I suggested. 'She'll be able to answer any questions that you might have.'

'What good will it do?' she replied. 'She can't tell me what's going to happen. At the moment, it feels like I'm never going to have the girls back with me ever again and it felt like everyone was so against me in that meeting.'

'People weren't against you,' I told her. 'You've been given a chance to prove yourself through a parenting assessment.'

But Zoe just seemed despondent.

After the end of the meeting, I had to quickly leave her so I had a chance to chat to Mrs Evans.

'I feel so awful having said those things in front of Zoe,' she sighed.

'You were just being honest,' I told her. 'It's important that Social Services have a true picture of what Coco's home life was like.'

We talked about Coco returning to school. It was Friday the following day so it made sense for her to wait and go in on Monday. Mrs Evans told me the start and finish times and where I could buy the uniform.

'I have lots of uniforms so if you can't get to the shops over the weekend then I can sort Coco out on Monday,' she told me.

'Thank you,' I smiled. 'We should be fine but I appreciate that.'

I then went to find Becky and we walked out of Social Services together. Reviews are always quite tiring but I felt emotionally drained after this one.

'Gosh, that was hard,' sighed Becky. 'I really did feel for Mum.'

I nodded in agreement. I couldn't imagine how it felt sitting there while a group of strangers talked about what they thought was best for your children while making it clear that your best hadn't been good enough. Yes, Zoe had made a bad judgement and put her children at risk, but she was clearly struggling financially without any support and now she had the threat of prison hanging over her head.

'Maggie, can I pop back home with you? I think you and I could do with having a supervision.' Becky asked.

I had supervision sessions with Becky once a month. They were a chance for me to catch up with her about my current placements, how I was feeling and if I needed help or any extra training with anything.

'Would you mind if we got a coffee and did it in my car instead?' I asked. 'The girls are with Louisa and I know as soon as I get back, Edie will want my attention and I want to make sure Coco and Lola are OK so I'll be too distracted.'

'Of course,' she said. 'I don't mind where we do it.'

So for the next half an hour, we sat in my car with a cappuccino and chatted. We talked about Amena and the fact that her mum, Hodan, was still in France looking after her aunt.

'It doesn't sound good to be honest,' Becky said. 'I think Hodan's sister's condition has deteriorated and she's in a pretty bad way.'

'Oh, that's sad,' I sighed.

I told Becky how Hodan called Amena every few days.

'Amena seems OK,' I said. 'She's a really lovely girl and she's very independent. She gets herself to school, does her homework no problem and never complains. She's really easy-going.'

'I'd like to have another catch up with her at some stage,' Becky said. 'Mum mentioned that perhaps Amena could get the ferry one weekend to France to visit her if she could get a cheap enough ticket.'

I wasn't sure about that as Amena was only fifteen, but I knew she was desperate to see her mum as it had been nearly a month.

Then we discussed Coco and Lola.

'They're doing OK everything considered,' I said. 'Everything's still so new for them and they've had so much change. Lola's still recovering from the pneumonia and not quite settled yet.'

'After today, I can see what you mean about Pamela,' Becky told me. 'She really seems to have it in for Zoe. It's almost like she's not prepared to give her a chance to prove herself.'

'Yes, I really felt for Zoe today,' I said.

I was pleased that Becky felt the same as I did about Pamela. I'd half expected Pamela to rein in her attitude in such an open forum but she hadn't and her comments had come across as harsh and unfair.

'I got the impression in the meeting that Heidi was getting frustrated with her too,' said Becky.

The IRO's role was to make sure that the children's needs were being met and she could pull a social worker up if she felt they were not doing their job properly.

Becky was so supportive and understanding. I knew I was lucky to have her and I always felt better after speaking to her.

'Let's keep in touch, Maggie, and I'd love to come round next week and actually meet the girls once they've settled in a bit more,' she told me.

'Of course,' I smiled. 'You're welcome any time.'

I waved Becky off and finally headed home. My body sagged with relief and tiredness as I pulled up outside my house. I'd just clicked the button to take my seatbelt off when I heard my phone ringing in my handbag on the front seat next to me. I picked it up to see Vicky's name on the screen.

'Hi, lovey,' I said, answering it. 'I'm about to walk in the front door from a LAC review so can I ring you back later? It's been a bit of a morning.'

Silence.

'Vicky?' I asked, assuming that she had pocket-dialled me by mistake. 'Are you there? Can you hear me?'

But suddenly on the other end of the line I heard a huge, guttural sob. My heart sank.

'Vicky,' I gasped. 'What's the matter? What's happened?'

She was crying so much that she could hardly get her words out.

'Take some deep breaths and try to tell me,' I soothed.

Vicky was always so calm and measured; I knew it must be something serious.

'Is it your mum? Has something happened to Marjorie?'

Vicky's mum was in her eighties and hadn't been very well recently.

'No, no,' she sobbed. 'It's not that. Mum's fine. It's the boys, Maggie. Something awful has happened.'

Her words chilled me to the bone.

She let out another heart-wrenching cry and all sorts of horrific scenarios ran through my head. Had they had an accident? Had one of them been hurt?

I could hear Vicky taking deep breaths to try to calm herself down as she struggled to get the words out.

'My supervising social worker has just rung me,' she wept. 'She told me not to go and pick the boys up from school later because allegations have been made against me.'

'What do you mean, "allegations"?' I asked. 'What sort of allegations?'

'I don't know,' she sighed. 'They're not allowed to tell me. All I know is that the boys aren't coming home, Maggie.'

Her voice quivered and she started to cry again, gulping sobs that meant she could barely catch her breath.

'But that's ridiculous!' I exclaimed.

'She just asked me to pack a bag for each for them and said

they won't be returning to me,' Vicky told me.

All she knew was that all three of the boys had gone to another foster carer but she wasn't allowed to know where or have any contact with them.

I was totally and utterly devastated for her.

'Vicky, I honestly don't know what to say,' I told her. 'It just sounds so unfair.'

Vicky had been a foster carer for over twenty years and she was one of the very best. In fact, she regularly helped to train new carers at her fostering agency. She was so loving and caring towards every child who came into her home, no matter what their background, and she had boundless energy and patience. She'd transformed those boys' lives over the past six months.

'I'm so sorry but I've got to go now,' I told her. 'I've been at a LAC review all morning and I need to see the girls and let Louisa get home.'

'It's OK, Maggie, I understand,' she sniffed.

'But listen, why don't you come round later after eight, when the younger girls are in bed and we can talk about this?'

'The boys are gone,' she wept. 'There's nothing more to say.'

'Well, just come round and I can keep you company,' I replied. 'We don't have to talk about it if you don't want to.'

Vicky was a single carer like me and I hated to think of her upset and at home all alone.

'Thank you,' she said meekly. 'I'll see how I feel.'

'Ring me if you need me and hopefully I'll see you later,' I told her. 'I'm so sorry, Vicky,' I added. 'I know how much those boys mean to you.'

'Thanks, Maggie,' she sighed.

As I walked up the front path, my head was spinning. I was so shocked and upset for Vicky. Allegations were something every foster carer dreaded. Of course, they always had to be investigated but it was often a slow and lengthy process and the harsh reality was that, in some cases, the allegations were found to be true and the children didn't return. Or it took so long for the allegations to be investigated, that by the time the foster carer was cleared, the children were already settled somewhere else and it was too disruptive to move them back.

I took a deep breath and turned the key in the lock to my front door. I knew I had to put on a brave face for the girls.

Thankfully, everything was calm at home. Louisa had already made everyone lunch and they were watching TV.

'How have they been?' I asked.

'They've been great,' she said. 'No bother at all.'

The rest of the day passed in a blur, my mind consumed by worries about Zoe and of course Vicky. She sent me a text later on that afternoon: *I will come round later. You were right, I could do with some company. The house is so quiet without the boys x*

Coco and Lola were in bed and Amena was in her room when there was a knock at the door at 8.30 p.m. Vicky stood on the doorstep. Her eyes were red-raw and puffy from hours of crying, and she looked utterly bereft.

I gave her a hug and she collapsed into my arms.

'I'm so sorry,' I told her.

'I just don't know what to do, Maggie,' she sobbed.

I led her into the kitchen and got her a cup of tea and a box of tissues.

She calmed down but I could see she was in shock.

'I just can't understand what the allegations are,' she said. 'I've been going over and over it all in my mind. I can't imagine what it is that I've supposed to have done to the boys and which of them has complained about me.'

I could see the not knowing was almost worse than the allegation itself. It was mental torture.

'Hopefully it can be sorted out quickly and you'll get the boys back soon,' I reassured her.

'Maggie, you and I know exactly how these things work,' she replied. 'Even when something's resolved quickly, it's normally still a few weeks. It just breaks my heart.'

'We will sort it out,' I reassured her.

We worked for separate fostering agencies but we'd both had training on how the allegation process worked and we both had colleagues who had been through it. Vicky's supervising social worker, Debbie, and her manager would attend a meeting called by the Local Authority Designated Officer (LADO). The LADO was the person who was notified when it had been alleged that someone who works with children may have behaved in a way that had harmed a child. The boys' social worker would attend the meeting along with someone from their schools and possibly the police as well. At this meeting they would agree whether to uphold the investigation and if so, how and by whom these allegations would be investigated. Vicky wouldn't be told when the LADO meeting was taking place but she'd be informed of the outcome afterwards.

'Hopefully LADO will decide the allegations are unsubstantiated,' I said.

Vicky shrugged.

'Who knows?' she sighed. 'The worst thing is not knowing what they are, so I can't even defend myself.'

'You need to give Fostering Network a call,' I told her. It was an organisation that was there to support foster carers if they had an allegation made against them. It wasn't just the emotional turmoil either. If you are a foster carer, as soon as an allegation is made against you and the children are removed from your care, your pay is immediately stopped and you're not allowed to foster any other children in the meantime. I knew foster carers who had gone bankrupt and lost their homes while false allegations against them were being investigated. It felt like a very unfair process sometimes. If a social worker ever had an allegation against them, it would still have to be investigated but they'd continue to get paid. Of course, children had to be listened to and any allegation had to be looked at and taken seriously, but it felt as if for the whole process you were deemed guilty until proven innocent – the opposite of our judicial system. Even if the allegation was not upheld, it still stayed on your fostering record and showed up on DBS (Disclosure and Barring Service) checks. If the allegation was upheld then you were never allowed to foster or work with children in any capacity again.

Vicky was a single carer with a mortgage to pay and I was worried about the fallout of her having no money coming in.

'How are you going to manage financially?' I asked her.

'I've got savings I can dip into but that's not going to last me long,' she sighed. 'I'll have to get another job – perhaps work in a shop or something.'

However, I knew that money was the last thing on her mind. I could see that she was going over and over everything in her head.

'I don't understand it, Maggie. Nothing's happened. One minute I was planning for a future with them with the Special Guardianship Order, and now they've been taken off me.'

I felt Vicky's pain – it was all just so unfair.

'What am I going to do, Maggie?' she asked plaintively. 'It feels like my heart has been ripped out.'

'It's going to be OK,' I soothed, giving her another hug.

But the reality was, I just didn't know.

TWELVE

A Special Guest

'Wow, don't you look smart,' I smiled as I helped Coco pull on her bottle green school jumper.

Over the weekend we'd been to the shops and got a couple of grey pleated skirts, some white polo shirts and green jumpers, black tights and a pair of shiny patent shoes. Coco's hair was freshly washed and I'd plaited it and tied it with bobbles with green bows on them.

'It's going to be lovely seeing all of your friends again and Mrs Evans is really looking forward to having you back,' I told her.

It was Coco's first day at school since she'd been taken into care and I was trying to keep everything upbeat and positive. My mind had been racing all weekend with worries about Vicky and Zoe, but I knew I had to put them to one side for a few hours and concentrate on Coco.

Thankfully she'd been fine so far this morning. She'd had breakfast, played with Lola and now seemed in a happy mood as I helped her get dressed into her uniform and then got them both into the car.

Finally, after a thirty-minute drive, I parked up on the street outside her school.

'Right then,' I said, turning round to Coco in the back seat of the car. 'Let's go in.'

She didn't say anything but I saw her bottom lip quiver.

'Oh my goodness,' I said. 'What is it, flower?'

Lola looked across from her car seat worriedly as tears spilled from Coco's eyes.

'Mummy always taked me to school,' she said in a quiet voice. 'I just want to go with my mummy.'

'We saw Mummy!' exclaimed Lola.

'Yeah, we went past Mummy,' added Coco. 'Why can't we go and get her?'

I was confused.

'What do you mean, we passed Mummy?' I asked, worried that Zoe had turned up at school unannounced.

'We just drived past our flat,' said Coco and Lola nodded.

'Oh, did we?' I replied. 'I didn't realise.'

I didn't know where the girls lived but if I had, I'd have made sure that we'd gone a different route. It was triggering and unsettling for them to see the home they shared with their mum and I reminded myself to get Zoe's address from Pamela to make sure I didn't go past there again.

I could understand Coco's upset and all I could do was acknowledge what she was saying. There was still the parenting assessment and the CPS (Crown Prosecution Service) decision to come, and I didn't want to give Coco false assurances that Zoe would be back to taking her to school again any time soon.

'I know things are different to normal and you must feel really sad,' I said. 'Mummy isn't able to take you to school at the moment but I'm here and I'd like to do it. Is that OK with you?'

Coco nodded sadly.

'It's not fair,' she said. 'It's taking a very long time for Mummy to talk to that lady.'

'I know,' I nodded. 'These things tend to take a long time because the grown-ups want to make sure that we get it right so we know that you and Lola are safe and happy.'

'But me and Lola *are* happy with Mummy,' Coco sighed.

It was so hard to explain things to young children in a way they could understand.

'Your mummy had to make some difficult choices and some of those choices didn't keep you and Lola safe,' I told her. 'It's important that she talks to Pamela so they can both work out how Mummy can do things a little bit differently next time.'

Coco shrugged and I wasn't sure if she had a clue what I was talking about. As far as she was concerned, I was the 'baddie' keeping her and Lola from seeing their mum. Children tended to view me as the one stopping them from seeing their birth parents as they didn't fully understand the role of the social worker or Social Services. It was hard sometimes but I knew it was easier for kids to have someone to blame and it almost became part of the job.

'At the moment, I'm going to be the one who takes you to school and picks you up but Mummy will see you and Lola soon,' I told her.

'Today?' asked Lola hopefully.

'I don't think it will be today but Pamela is going to make sure that you both see Mummy this week.'

I knew how keen Heidi had been at the meeting for Pamela to get regular contact sessions organised. That seemed to appease Coco for now and although she was quiet, she let me walk her to her classroom and she went in without any problems.

When Lola and I had driven home, Pamela rang me.

'Is everything OK?' I asked her after I'd updated her about the school drop-off.

'Not really, Maggie,' she sighed. 'It's very easy for the IRO to say we have to have contact three times a week but has she tried finding a contact centre in the area with a vacant slot between 3.30 and 5.30 p.m.? How am I supposed to fit contact in three times a week if there are no contact workers to supervise it and no contact centres to do it in?'

With Coco back at school, contact had to be outside of school hours as the local authority weren't keen on children missing their lessons.

I let Pamela finish her rant.

'I know it can be tricky,' I told her. 'I've supervised contact sessions in the past when there's been the need so I'm happy to do one of the sessions at my house each week if that helps?'

There was a pause.

'Actually, that would be great,' replied Pamela. 'It has to be done properly though, you know. You'll have to write up an in-depth report after each session and make sure Zoe is fully supervised at all times.'

I could feel my hackles rising. I took a deep breath and tried not to get too annoyed.

'Pamela, I've been doing this for over twenty years but if you're worried, perhaps you'd like to have a chat with my supervising social worker to decide if I'm up to the job or not?' I said to her.

'Oh no, no I didn't mean that,' said Pamela, quickly backtracking. 'Thank you, and I'll definitely take you up on your offer. It would really help.'

To be honest, I'd suggested it because I knew it would be nicer for both Zoe and the girls to have contact at my house. Things would be a lot more relaxed than at the contact centre. Zoe wasn't seen as a risk as such because she hadn't been violent or abusive to the children – they could just spend quality time together.

'Would there be any flexibility around timings?' I asked Pamela. 'I obviously have to think about the needs of my other placement.'

'Yes, of course,' she said. 'We'd be happy to fit in around you.'

I knew Amena was really flexible but I thought it would be nice for Zoe to be able to stay later and have the opportunity to carry out some normal activities with the girls such as putting them to bed, giving them a bath or reading them a story. I knew Coco and Lola would like that too.

I'd only had Pamela's version and I still hadn't heard the full story from Zoe herself, but my instincts about her had always been that she was a loving, caring mother who was struggling for money and had made some bad decisions forced by her circumstances. Having contact sessions at my house would enable me to see whether that was the case and give me more of an insight into Zoe and her parenting. If I was going to fight her corner, I needed to know what the true picture was.

We organised the first contact session at my house for the following day. That gave Pamela more time to try to organise another session at a contact centre later in the week.

'I would normally come along to the first one, Maggie, but I've got a meeting tomorrow,' she told me. 'I'll give Zoe your address and she can find her own way there.'

Even though Zoe seemed devoted to her girls, there was no guarantee that she would turn up for contact and I didn't want Coco and Lola to get too worked up or excited. So I didn't tell them the news until I picked Coco up from school the following day and I'd had a text from Pamela confirming that Zoe was on her way.

The car was always a good place to have important conversations or relay information as it was hard to sit young children down and expect them to concentrate.

'Guess what?' I smiled. 'We've got to get home really quickly today because your mummy's coming to my house to see you.'

Coco and Lola looked confused.

'We're not going to the place with the toys?' asked Coco, looking slightly disappointed.

'Not this time,' I told her. 'But you can show Mummy the toys at my house and she might even stay and have tea with us.'

The girls looked across at each other and grinned.

'I can show her the special tap and Lola, you can show her the toy castle,' smiled Coco. 'And she can see our bedroom.'

Lola nodded, her green eyes shining with excitement.

I could see they couldn't wait to get back.

'Is Mummy here yet?' Coco asked as we pulled up outside.

'Not just yet,' I told her. 'She's coming in a little while.'

I got them a beaker of orange squash and some biscuits but neither of them could sit still. In the end, they both insisted on standing by the front window to wait for Zoe.

'She might not come for a while as she's got to get a couple of buses,' I warned them but they insisted.

Fifteen minutes later, there was a huge shriek.

'She's here!' yelled Coco and I heard the thundering of little feet in the hallway as both girls bolted to the front door.

I walked through from the kitchen to open it.

Zoe stood on the doorstep. She looked pale and exhausted and was shivering with cold. She was wearing holey jeans and a thin jacket even though it was freezing outside. Her face lit up when she saw the girls and they threw themselves into her arms.

'Let Mummy come in and get out of the cold,' I told them gently.

I could see Zoe was nervous as she walked into the hallway and looked around.

'You've got a beautiful home,' she said to me.

'Thank you.'

I felt guilty thinking about the bare, cold flat the duty social worker had described and I didn't want to make Zoe feel any worse than she already did.

The girls tugged on her arms.

'Mummy, Mummy, come and see mine and Lola's bedroom,' begged Coco.

'Mummy, come look at the toys,' shouted Lola. 'I like the castle and the dollies best.'

Zoe stood there awkwardly, looking unsure about what to do first.

'How about we take Mummy into the kitchen and make her a cup of tea to help warm her up,' I smiled. 'I know you're excited, girls, but she's here for a while so there's plenty of time to show her everything.'

'Thank you,' said Zoe, who looked hesitant.

We went into the kitchen and I could see her taking it all in.

'What a lovely bright room,' she said.

'And there's a garden too,' said Coco, leading her over to the patio doors and pointing to the lawn.

'And Mummy, look at all the toys,' she shouted, as she ran to the toy cupboard and flung open the doors.

'Yeah, there's the castle,' smiled Lola. 'And the dollies and the bricks and the jigsaw and the cars.'

'Wow, I see what you mean,' nodded Zoe. 'There are so many toys.'

'Yes, Maggie has lots and lots,' nodded Coco.

I knew how overwhelming it all must be for Zoe and I didn't want to force her into opening up to me or feeling like she had to chat. She was here to spend time with the girls, after all. By the time the kettle had boiled, she was sitting on the floor playing with the toy castle with them.

I think it's always nice for parents and children to do an activity together so I suggested that Zoe and the girls do some baking.

Coco and Lola already knew exactly where everything was. Coco ran to my big kitchen cupboard and pulled it open.

'Look Mummy,' she told her. 'Look at all the food Maggie's got in here.'

'And there's more there too,' she said, pointing at the fridge. 'And when she goes to the shop, she just buys what she wants with a special card.'

I could see Zoe didn't know what to say in response and I quickly changed the subject.

'Here are some mixing bowls and a spoon each and some

scales to weigh your ingredients,' I told the girls.

I gave them a recipe for a simple chocolate sponge cake.

'Gosh, I haven't done this in years and years,' said Zoe as she showed them how to measure out flour and stir in the sugar and milk. 'I used to do this when I was little with my mum.'

'Is that the one in heaven?' asked Coco, and Zoe nodded.

'You never met Nanny Kerry but she used to make lovely cakes,' said Zoe sadly.

'We've never done baking with you, have we, Mummy?' asked Coco.

'No, we haven't,' nodded Zoe.

I tidied up the toys and folded up some ironing while Zoe and the girls were over on the other side of the kitchen. I watched them out of the corner of my eye and it was lovely to see the relaxed body language between them.

'You're getting flour all over your hair, Lo Lo,' laughed Zoe, tucking her daughter's long golden hair behind her ear.

'And you've got flour on your nose, missy,' she said to Coco.

'Me want flour on my nose, Mummy,' replied Lola in a baby voice.

Zoe playfully dusted a bit of flour on her nose too and both girls giggled.

I could sense there was a natural affection between her and the girls. I had seen enough parents in the past who had put on an act for social workers during contact sessions. But you could normally tell from the child's body language when it was fake – the child would be confused, stiff and surprised. I'd even seen some children flinch when their birth parent was seemingly giving them affection. But I could see how relaxed Coco and Lola were around Zoe and there was a warmth and

139

ease between the three of them.

One thing I did notice was Zoe hungrily tucking into the plate of biscuits that I'd put out as an after-school snack for the girls. She must have realised I was watching her because she suddenly flinched.

'Sorry,' she said, her cheeks burning red. 'I should have asked.'

'Not at all,' I smiled. 'Please, tuck in. I can make you a sandwich or some toast if you'd like?'

'Oh no, there's no need,' she said, clearly embarrassed. 'It's fine. I was just being greedy.'

But her bony face and frail body didn't convince me.

'Well, I hope you have a big appetite because I've made a huge lasagne for tea,' I smiled.

'Thank you,' she said, and I'm sure I noticed tears in her eyes.

Finally, the cake was in the oven and the girls were busy playing so I made Zoe another cup of tea.

'You've got such a lovely house,' she sighed. 'And the girls seem so happy here.'

'They're happy because they're with their mummy,' I smiled. 'They've been so excited about seeing you. They were standing by the window for ages waiting for you to arrive.'

She took a sip of tea.

'I'm glad that we could do this here,' Zoe told me. 'All I think about is the girls and I can picture where they are now.'

She paused.

'I just wish I could give them everything that you've given them. Toys, food . . . Coco looks so smart in her school uniform.'

I really didn't want to make her feel inadequate.

'Anyone can buy children "stuff",' I told her. 'But it's their mummy that they want. They might have material things but emotionally their bond is with you.'

Zoe nodded but she didn't look convinced.

The two hours flew by and after dinner it was time for Zoe to leave. This was always the part that I dreaded.

'I'm afraid Mummy has to go now,' I told Coco and Lola.

They clung to Zoe's legs and sobbed. I could see Zoe was doing her best to hold back her own tears.

'Please stay with us,' pleaded Lola tearfully.

'Don't worry, Mummy will be coming again soon,' I told them. 'And next time we can see if Mummy can stay and give you a bath.'

The girls' faces lit up.

'That would be nice, wouldn't it?' smiled Zoe.

'Yes,' nodded Coco. 'And Maggie's bath is warm and bubbly. She's got a special tap and hot water comes out of it.'

'That sounds lovely,' said Zoe, giving her a sad smile.

While they'd been baking, I had taken a photo of them and printed out three copies. I handed one to Zoe and gave one to each of the girls.

'Here's a photo for Mummy to take with her and you've both got one to put in your bedroom.'

'I'll give your picture big kisses tonight, girls,' Zoe told them.

'We can give Mummy a kiss night night too,' smiled Lola, pressing the photo against her lips.

'I know, we could all give our pictures a big kiss at seven o'clock tonight,' smiled Coco.

'That's a great idea,' I told her. 'In that case, Mummy needs to go now to make sure she's back in time to give your photo a kiss goodnight.'

It was the perfect distraction and the girls had a little smile on their faces as they gave their mummy a hug and waved goodbye.

I could see Zoe was still doing her best not to cry.

'Thank you, Maggie,' she whispered as she lingered on the doorstep. 'Thank you for looking after them the way I couldn't.'

Then she disappeared down the path into the darkness.

THIRTEEN

A Vicious Circle

As Vicky sobbed down the phone to me, my heart sank.

For the past few days, she had been torturing herself about the allegations that had been made against her. The three boys hadn't returned to her care and she had been stuck at home, worrying and imagining the worst. Now one of the things she'd been fearing had happened.

'I've just got back from the police station,' she wept. 'They interviewed me under caution for child cruelty.'

'Oh Vicky, I am·sorry. That must have been really tough for you.'

'It was,' she replied. 'It's just all so upsetting. It was terrifying too – I've never been interviewed by the police before.'

I couldn't help but think of how many similarities there were between what was happening to her and to Zoe.

'Did you find out any more about what you've been accused of and who's actually accused you?' I asked her.

Vicky let out a loud sob.

'Yes. It's just awful, Maggie. It was Robert.'

Robert, thirteen, was the eldest of the three brothers Vicky had been fostering.

'Apparently he told his teacher that I'd lost my temper on a couple of occasions and slapped him,' she told me. 'I just don't understand it. Why would he make something up like that?'

'I honestly don't know,' I replied.

'I've never, ever laid a finger on any child,' she added. 'You know that. I'd never do anything to hurt the boys.'

'It's so ridiculous. Hopefully Social Services will realise pretty quickly that it's not true,' I reassured her.

'I hoped the same,' she told me. 'But the worst thing is, Maggie, John has apparently backed him up and agreed with his story. He said he'd seen me slapping Robert. I'm so upset. Why would a ten-year-old say such a thing? Why would either of them make up something like that?'

I was as puzzled as Vicky and didn't have any answers. The only thing that I could think was that it was a subconscious reaction against Vicky wanting to get a Special Guardianship Order to look after the boys full-time. Perhaps Robert had made these allegations up because he was scared of getting too close to Vicky? Perhaps he was worried he was going to be rejected by Vicky so he was pushing her away?

'I keep thinking about little Grant,' said Vicky. 'He's suffering because of his brothers' lies. I miss his cuddles and the way he used to twiddle with my hair when he was tired. I hate being at home now, Maggie. The house is so quiet without the three of them.'

'At least you know what you're accused of now, so you can try to defend yourself,' I told her.

'It's just the unknown,' she sighed. 'I don't know how long it's going to take to be able to clear my name.

'Or even *if* I'll be able to clear my name.'

'You will,' I reassured her.

It was a horrendous thing for Vicky to go through and I felt helpless. All I could do was stay positive and be there for her when she needed to talk. I knew my friend and I knew that she wasn't capable of physically hurting a child.

'In my head I keep thinking, what if I'm charged with child cruelty? Could I end up going to prison or getting a criminal record?'

'I'm sure it won't come to that,' I told her, echoing the words I'd said to Zoe the previous night.

A few days later, Pamela managed to organise another contact session back at Oak Lodge so I took the girls there after school. I'd not heard anything from Zoe since that last meeting. Seeing her now, I thought she looked tired but she gave me a smile and was pleased to see the girls as always.

Pamela pulled me to one side.

'I know Heidi was obsessed with contact three times a week but I have tried and tried and I can't find the space,' she sighed.

'I honestly don't mind having a second session at my house at the weekend,' I told her. 'I think it went well last time and I know the girls liked having their mum around.'

'Well, it's better than nothing I suppose,' she said. 'I'll let Zoe know.'

When I told the girls, they were excited.

'Can Mummy stay and give us a bath like you said last time?' asked Coco.

'Mummy do stories,' said Lola.

'I'm sure she'd love that,' I smiled.

When she arrived at my house for the contact session, I mentioned it to Zoe.

'That would be amazing,' she smiled.

I always had to be in the same room as her and the girls as I was supervising the session and couldn't leave Zoe on her own with them. But rather than sit there and watch them, as tended to happen with the workers at the contact centre, I always tried to be busy doing something so that it seemed normal.

After dinner, Zoe took them upstairs for a bath. I let her take charge while I tasked myself with sorting out the towel cupboard in the bathroom.

I was hoping Coco wouldn't make a big deal about the hot tap as I didn't want Zoe to feel inadequate, but as soon as they walked into the bathroom, she led her towards the bath.

'Mummy, look at this,' she said, pointing to the taps. 'This one has warm water coming out of it. We don't need to have a magic wash at Maggie's. Can we get one of them at our house?

Zoe smiled.

'Wow, that sounds lovely, Coco, and I'll try my very best to get us one of those at our flat,' she said to her.

Zoe put on a brave face in front of the girls but I could see the sadness in her eyes. I knew it must have been hard for her when they kept pointing out things they didn't have at home.

I was struck once again by how natural Zoe and the girls were with each other and I could see the affection between them – the little ruffles of their hair, the kisses and the cuddles, the ease with which the girls plonked themselves on Zoe's lap so she could dry them and help them into their pyjamas. The way their legs and arms naturally intertwined with hers and how they twiddled with her hair. I could tell Coco and Lola just wanted to be near their mum all the time and Zoe was savouring every chance to be close to her girls.

'I think it might be story time now,' I smiled when both girls were in their pyjamas.

They all trooped to their bedroom and I followed with the laundry basket full of clean clothes. While they did stories, I put the washing away in their drawers.

Zoe and the girls snuggled up together on Coco's single bed.

'Do you need any books?' I asked them.

'We don't need books do we, girls?' asked Zoe and they both grinned and shook their heads.

'Mummy makes up our stories,' said Coco proudly.

I kept myself busy while Zoe told them a story about two sisters who flew around the world visiting lots of countries and feeding lots of animals. Coco and Lola snuggled into her, laughing and giggling and looking completely enthralled.

'Our mummy does better stories than you,' Coco told me.

'Coco, please don't be rude,' Zoe told her.

'That's OK,' I smiled. 'It's true. That's because Mummy knows what you like far better than me.'

It was coming up to 7.30 p.m. and I could see the girls were getting sleepy. I also wanted to go downstairs and spend some time with Amena, who was watching TV in the front room.

'Time to say goodnight to Mummy,' I told the girls gently.

'I don't have to kiss your picture tonight,' said Coco, pointing to the photo that I had printed out the last time Zoe was here.

'No,' smiled Zoe. 'You get a real-life Mummy this time.'

'Mummy here in the morning?' Lola asked hopefully as she kissed and cuddled her.

'I wish I could be, sweetheart,' she said. 'But I'm afraid I have to go back home after you've gone to bed.'

'Mummy will see you again soon,' I reassured Lola.

Thankfully the girls weren't as tearful this time. Perhaps saying goodnight seemed more normal and they didn't have to watch Zoe go out of the front door. However, I could see Zoe was struggling to hold back her own tears as we walked downstairs.

'Saying goodbye never gets any easier, does it?' I said sympathetically.

'No,' she said, wiping her eyes. 'I try to put a brave face on in front of the girls but I'll never get used to it.'

I felt bad about making her leave straight away when she was upset so I came up with a suggestion.

'Would you like a quick of cup of tea before you go as it's a bit chilly out there tonight?' I asked her. 'I'm sorry I can't give you a lift home but I can't leave the girls.'

Zoe looked hesitant.

'Is that allowed?' she asked. 'I don't want to be accused of breaking any rules.'

'Of course it is,' I smiled. 'Don't worry, it's not part of the contact session.'

As we walked into the kitchen, I noticed the big casserole dish of macaroni cheese on the side.

'We've got so much left over from dinner,' I sighed. 'I don't know what I'm going to do with it all. Would you like to take some home with you?'

I could tell Zoe was about to say no and then she hesitated.

'OK, thank you,' she said.

I got the impression Zoe often went hungry and I had almost a motherly instinct to feed her up and get some nourishment inside her.

She perched on a stool at the breakfast bar while I put the kettle on.

'Was it nice being able to bathe your girls and put them to bed?' I asked her as I handed her a steaming mug of tea.

'It was lovely,' she replied. 'It just felt normal, you know, although we don't have a bath at our house.'

'Have you lived round here for a long time?' I asked her but Zoe shook her head. 'Have you got family around here?'

'No,' she shrugged. 'My mum died when I was a teenager and my stepdad was useless. He quickly moved on from Mum and got married again. I stayed with him until I was seventeen then left as soon as I could. My stepmother wasn't a very nice woman and we haven't been in touch since,' she said.

'I hope you don't mind me asking this, but do the girls ever see their dad?'

Zoe shook her head.

'He's from Spain and I met him when he was over here working. When Lola was born, he decided he was too young to be tied down and he hasn't been in the girls' lives since. I wouldn't even know where to find him,' she told me.

'Gosh, you really have been on your own with little or no support,' I said.

'It's always just been me and my girls,' she shrugged.

Up until now, Zoe had been very closed off so it was nice that she trusted me enough to start opening up to me. She talked about how, when the girls were little, she survived on benefits.

'But it got harder and harder,' she told me. 'The price of things was going up and the benefits were going down so I thought I'd try to get a job.'

She'd even moved them from a small town to a city to increase her chances of finding work.

'I couldn't get a council house because we weren't considered a priority so I was put on a long waiting list,' she told me. 'I had to find a flat through a private landlord. It was the cheapest one I could find that would take housing benefit,' she said. 'But I soon realised that it was cheap for a reason.'

She described how their flat was damp and cold and had mould on the walls. 'We all sleep in the living room because the girls were getting ill. I kept complaining to the landlord but he never did anything. He knew I was trapped – I couldn't leave because I'd never find anything cheaper. He even had the cheek to put the rent up so my benefit wasn't covering it any more and I was in arrears.'

Zoe described how she couldn't afford childcare in the day for Lola and struggled to get work. The only thing she could find was a cash-in-hand job cleaning offices at night three times a week.

'It was all I could get so I took it because my benefits weren't enough to live on,' she told me. 'I had no one to look after the girls so I had to take them with me at first. But it wasn't fair on them as it was affecting their sleep and then my boss found out and said he'd get rid of me.

'That's why I did what I did. I'm so ashamed but I was running out of options. I made the stupid decision to leave them at night while I went out to work. I hated doing it, I really did, but I couldn't see any way out. If I lost my job, I couldn't afford my rent, and then we'd be out on the streets. I wouldn't be able to afford food and I couldn't bear the thought of my children going hungry.'

I could hear the desperation in Zoe's voice and my heart went out to her.

'It sounds like an impossible situation,' I nodded.

'I did the best I could,' she sighed, her eyes filling with tears. 'Every day felt like a struggle. I was stuck in a vicious circle. If I paid my rent then I couldn't afford to buy tokens for the electric. If I paid my bills then we didn't have enough to buy food. It was exhausting. I did my best to make sure the girls always ate something at least,' she sobbed. 'I vowed I would never let them go without. I always found a solution. Sometimes I did things I'm not proud of to get by.'

'You mean shoplifting?' I asked and she nodded, her cheeks burning with shame.

'I know it's wrong but recently it was the only way we could afford to eat by the end of the week,' she said. 'That night I got done, Lola was burning up and I couldn't afford to go to the pharmacy. What kind of a mother can't afford to buy medicine for her child? I'm just so ashamed.'

She shook her head and sobbed.

My heart ached for her.

'I'm so sorry for everything that you've been through,' I told her, putting my hand on hers. 'It sounds like you were doing the very best you could.'

'Honestly I was,' Zoe nodded. 'But I've realised now that my best isn't good enough.'

It felt so sad to see how little she thought of herself.

'Have you told Pamela and the police everything that you've just told me?' I asked her.

'I've tried to,' she shrugged. 'But they're not interested in the "why". They just want to focus on the fact that I left my children home alone.

'I know I did that,' she sighed. 'But at the time I didn't feel like I had any other options. Everything had got on top of me.'

Zoe suddenly looked at the clock on the wall.

'I'm sorry,' she said, jumping up and wiping away her tears. 'I know you don't want to hear my sob story. I'm way over time and you've got your other foster child to see to. I'd better go.'

'Don't feel like you have to,' I told her. 'You're welcome to stay for another cuppa?'

'No, I need to head back as I have a couple of buses to catch. I've probably said way too much.'

I followed Zoe out into the hallway and she grabbed her coat from the banister. As she put it on, she pulled out her phone from her jacket pocket. The screen was smashed and it had clearly seen better days.

'Oh, I've missed a call,' she said, sounding worried. 'I'm just going to listen to this voicemail.'

I nodded.

I could see Zoe's face change as she listened to the message. She looked terrified.

'Is everything OK?' I asked her but she shook her head and burst into tears.

'Hey,' I soothed. 'What is it? What's happened?'

I could see that her hands were shaking.

'It was the police. They left a message to say I'm going to be charged with child endangerment. They said I've got to go to court and say whether I'm pleading guilty or not.'

It was all her worst fears come true.

'I'm going to go to prison,' she mumbled. 'I'm going to be locked up for years and I'm never going to get my girls back.'

'I'm so sorry,' I told her. 'It will be OK. You'll qualify for legal aid so you can get a solicitor to help you.'

But I could see that nothing I said was going to help ease Zoe's distress.

'Please stay for another cup of tea,' I urged her. 'I don't want to send you home in this state.'

'I can't,' she said, turning towards the front door. 'You've done so much for me tonight already and been so kind. I have to go now.'

And before I could say another word, she opened the front door and disappeared off into the cold, dark night.

FOURTEEN

Breaking Point

I'd just got back from the school drop-off and Vicky had popped round for a coffee. I wanted to help take her mind off the allegations and Lola provided a good distraction.

'I'm really missing being around children,' she smiled sadly as she played dolls with Lola on the kitchen floor.

'I'll put the kettle on,' I told her.

I was just getting the coffee out of the cupboard when my mobile rang.

Zoe's name flashed up on the screen.

Pamela had asked me if it was OK to pass my number to her in case she needed to let me know about arrangements for contact.

'Hi, Zoe,' I said cheerfully. 'I was just thinking about you. How are you feeling?'

It was a couple of days since she'd been at my house for contact and had left in a distressed state.

'Not good,' she said. 'I haven't slept a wink. I keep thinking about having to go to court and being sent to prison.'

Her voice was quiet and strangely emotionless and I could hardly hear her as there was lots of background noise.

'Where are you?' I asked her. 'It sounds like you're somewhere windy.'

But she didn't answer my question.

'I can't bear the thought of going to prison and never seeing the girls again,' she said. 'They're my world, Maggie.'

'I know they are, Zoe,' I said. 'But even if the worst-case scenario happens and you do go to prison, you'll always be able to see the girls. Social Services will make sure that you have contact with them.'

'I don't want them coming to see me in prison,' she replied. 'I would never ever put them through that.'

'You could be worrying yourself silly for nothing,' I said. 'Chances are, you won't even go to prison. When the judge hears about everything that you've been through, they will understand about the hard choices you had to make. You were in an impossible situation and you felt like there was no way out – the court will see that.'

'You can't guarantee that,' she told me.

I had to be honest with her.

'No, I can't,' I said. 'But whatever happens, we will work this out.'

Zoe went quiet again. I heard a car engine revving and a plane in the background. She was clearly outside somewhere.

'I've got to go to court in a few weeks to make a plea,' she sighed. 'I never thought I would be someone who had to go to court. I can't bear it.'

She paused again.

'I've been thinking and there's something I need to tell you,' she continued. 'I've decided that the girls are better off with you. You can give them everything that I can't.'

'Zoe, don't be daft, that's simply not true,' I said firmly. 'They want you – their mummy.'

'They'd have a much better life without me – food on the table, warm baths, comfy beds,' she said dejectedly. 'Baking, drawing, days out, lots of toys . . .' Her voice trailed off. 'I can't give them any of that stuff.'

'Zoe, they don't care about any of those material things,' I replied. 'They just want their mummy.'

She went quiet again.

'Zoe?' I asked. 'Are you still there?'

There was something about the tone of her voice and the way that this conversation was going that was really starting to worry me.

'Zoe?' I asked. 'Please talk to me.'

'Maggie, I want you to do something for me,' she said.

'Yes, of course,' I replied. 'What is it?'

'Can you tell the girls that I love them and I always will,' she said. 'They're the best thing that's ever happened to me and I don't deserve them.'

There was something about the way she was speaking now that unnerved me. It was almost robotic.

The hairs on the back of my neck stood on end.

'Zoe, where are you?' I asked her.

'That doesn't matter,' she said blankly. 'I just want you to promise me that you'll tell the girls that I love them. 'They're OK aren't they, Maggie?'

'They're absolutely fine,' I said. 'They're looking forward to seeing you at contact again in a couple of days.'

'They don't need contact with me,' she said. 'You see I've finally worked it out, Maggie. I'm better off out of the picture. I don't deserve them, I'm not good enough.'

'Zoe, that's simply not true,' I told her. 'The girls need you.'

I could see Vicky looking at me from over the other side of the kitchen, concern etched on her face.

'Everything OK?' she mouthed.

I shrugged my shoulders.

I could still hear a lot of noise in the background and there was a car beeping.

'What's all that commotion?' I asked her.

'Oh, I'm just in a car park,' she told me.

'But you don't have a car, Zoe,' I replied, growing more and more concerned by the minute.

'I'm just sat here on the top floor, admiring the view,' she said blankly. 'I can see everything from up here. It's so high up and windy and when I look over the edge, it makes my tummy go all funny. I can even see the Social Services building. I never want to step foot in that place again.'

Panic surged through me. I was convinced hearing the way that Zoe was talking that there was something dreadfully wrong.

My mind was racing, desperately thinking of where she could be. I remembered there was a big multi-storey car park over the other side of town near Social Services.

My instincts were telling me that Zoe was in danger of hurting herself and I knew I needed to get someone to her and quickly. But I had to keep her on the phone and keep her talking.

I waved frantically at Vicky playing with Lola and beckoned her to come over.

'What is it?' she whispered.

I reached for the notebook and pen on the work surface near me and quickly scribbled something down.

Zoe – girls' mum on phone. Worried she's going 2 hurt herself. Plse call 999 on yr mobile. I need to keep her talking.

'Where is she?' whispered Vicky.

I quickly wrote – *Think multi-storey car park in town, one near Social Services. Top floor. She's talking about being sat on edge.*

Vicky nodded, ran over to her bag and quickly grabbed her mobile.

'I'll be back in a minute, sweetheart,' she told Lola, who was happily playing and she quickly disappeared out of the kitchen out of earshot.

I swallowed the panic in my throat. Even though I wasn't calm, I knew I needed to sound like I was to Zoe. I couldn't let her hang up on me, I had to keep her talking.

Now she was ranting about how scared she was about having to go to court.

'Nobody knows what's going to happen in court,' I told Zoe. 'But you're working with Social Services so that will be seen in your favour. You've got two lovely little girls and you've got to keep fighting for them, Zoe.'

'I don't think I can,' she sighed. 'You see, I'm so tired, Maggie. So, so tired.'

'Everything seems so much worse when you've not been sleeping,' I told her. 'Have you been to see your GP?'

'What's the point? No one can help me.'

'We all want to help you, Zoe,' I told her. 'We're all here for you and the girls. After what you told me the other night, it's no wonder that you were forced to do what you did. Everyone will realise that you need help and support, not locking up.'

Zoe gave a deep sigh.

'But no one sees that,' she said, her voice cracking with emotion. 'Pamela thinks I'm the world's worst mother. I can see how she looks at me with such disgust.'

'Anyone who sees you with your girls can see what a good mum you are and how much you love them. Pamela will come to realise that in time too.'

'It's not enough,' she said blankly. 'They're better off without me in their lives.'

'Zoe, please listen to me,' I said firmly. 'Coco and Lola need you. They love you so much.'

I was repeating the same things over and over.

While I was talking, I was desperately staring at the kitchen door, willing Vicky to come back in and tell me help was on its way to Zoe.

I kept on talking, saying anything I could to keep her on the phone and safe.

I could hear her softly crying now.

'Zoe, are you still there?' I asked her.

'Yes,' she sobbed. 'I'm here. I just want all of this to be over, Maggie.'

My heart thumped out of my chest. I wanted to scream and shout at her not to do anything stupid but I took a deep breath to calm my nerves and began to talk.

I told her how much Coco and Lola loved her and how, when they saw her, their little faces lit up.

'Remember how delighted they were the other night when

you gave them a bath?' I smiled. 'There are so many more of those happy times to come.'

I talked about how much the girls had enjoyed baking with her the other day.

'No one can make them light up the way you do. They love your cuddles and the way you make up stories to tell them. They're always asking about you and when they can come home.'

'They'll soon forget me if I'm in prison,' sighed Zoe.

'They will *never* forget you,' I told her. 'You're their mummy and they love you so, so much.'

A few seconds later, the kitchen door flew open and Vicky came running in.

Called 999, she wrote on the pad. *Emergency services on way.*

I gave her a thumbs-up.

'Thank you,' I mouthed.

But there was no time to relax. Zoe was ranting now. She wasn't really talking to me.

'I just want all of this to end,' she kept saying.

'It will be over soon,' I replied. 'We're going to help you sort all of this out and you have your parenting assessment, which I'm sure you're going to pass with flying colours.'

'Not if Pamela's got anything to do with it,' replied Zoe.

I was getting more and more desperate now. I'd never ever been in this situation before and I'd never had any training on it.

'Maggie, I have to go now,' Zoe said wearily.

'No!' I shouted. 'Please stay. I need you to stay on the phone and keep talking to me. Please listen to me, Zoe,' I begged. 'Coco and Lola need you. No one can ever replace you and you are so important to those little girls.

'Whatever you're thinking right now, please don't do it. Please come round and see me and we can have a cup of tea like we did the other night and talk about this. I'm begging you, for Coco and Lola's sake, please don't do anything silly.'

Zoe didn't respond. However, much to my relief, I heard sirens in the background.

Thank goodness, I thought.

I heard Zoe let out a loud, guttural sob.

'I have to go,' she murmured.

'Zoe!' I yelled. 'Zoe? Please don't hang up. Are you there?'

Then the line went dead and finally there was silence.

FIFTEEN

The Battle Begins

Vicky and I stared at each other in shock.

'What the heck just happened?' she asked me.

'I heard sirens in the background and Zoe went quiet and then the phone went dead,' I told her, panic in my voice. 'Oh, Vicky, what if they didn't get to her in time? What if she saw the police coming and did something stupid?'

All the adrenalin and the shock from the past twenty minutes hit me and I burst into tears.

'I couldn't live with myself if anything has happened to Zoe,' I sobbed. 'How on earth could I tell the girls?'

Now it was Vicky's turn to comfort me.

'She'll be OK,' she soothed, giving me a hug. 'The police were there and they told me they were sending an ambulance too. They're trained in this kind of thing – they'll know exactly what to do.'

'I know,' I sobbed. 'But what if they didn't get to her in time?'

'They will have done,' she told me and I desperately wanted to believe her.

I glanced over at Lola who was thankfully still engrossed in her dollies and hadn't noticed the commotion or that I was upset.

'I'll never forgive myself if something happens to her,' I said. 'I was so shocked; I didn't know what to do for the best. All I could think was I had to keep her on the phone and keep talking to her. But what if I said the wrong thing?'

'Maggie, you did the very best you could in the moment,' Vicky told me. 'Besides, you don't even know for sure that she was intending to hurt herself.'

'I know she didn't explicitly say it, but the way she was talking, it gave me chills,' I shuddered. 'The tone of her voice had changed too. It just felt like she'd given up. And what on earth would she be doing on the top floor of a car park?'

It just didn't bear thinking about.

I knew I needed to call my supervising social worker and let her know what had happened.

'I must ring Becky but I don't want to use my phone in case the police or someone calls about Zoe,' I said.

'Remember I called them from my phone, Maggie, so it's probably me they'll ring,' said Vicky.

'Oh yes, you're right,' I told her. 'I'm not thinking straight.'

I got Lola settled in front of the TV and Vicky made us both a coffee while I called Becky.

'Something's just happened with Zoe,' I told her.

As I recounted her phone call, I couldn't stop myself from bursting into tears again.

'Oh my goodness, poor woman,' she sighed. 'I really hope she's OK.'

'Me too. I just didn't know what to do. I could tell something was horribly wrong.'

'It sounds like you did everything that you could at the time to help her,' Becky told me. 'You must have been terrified, Maggie. I'm not surprised you're shaken up.'

'I must admit, now the adrenalin has gone, I feel a bit shaky,' I replied. 'I'm just desperate to know that Zoe is OK.'

Becky said that she would contact Pamela and let her know.

'I don't think it will do you any good to have to go over it all again,' she told me. 'I'm glad Vicky's with you and please let me know when you have any updates about Zoe.'

'I will do,' I said.

I felt sick as I looked at the clock. It had been over half an hour since Zoe had hung up on me and we'd not heard anything yet. All I could do was pray the police had reached her in time and she was OK.

'It was probably just a cry for help,' Vicky reassured me. 'She probably didn't intend to hurt herself.'

'I don't honestly know,' I sighed. 'It was like she'd lost all hope. She's not been sleeping either, which stops you from being able to think straight. I wasn't prepared to take any chances.'

'You did the right thing,' Vicky told me. 'The police were taking it very seriously.'

I thought about little Lola watching cartoons in the front room and Coco at school and my heart ached for them. I could see how much they loved Zoe and the thought of having to tell them that something had happened to her was just unbearable. The tears flowed down my cheeks.

'I'm sorry,' I told Vicky as she handed me a coffee. 'You know I'm not normally a big crier.'

'You're in shock, Maggie,' she told me, putting her hand on my arm.

As I sipped my coffee, I stared at Vicky's phone on the worktop in front of us, willing it to ring and for someone to tell me that everything was OK.

But, a few minutes later, it was *my* mobile that rang. I pounced on it.

'Maggie, it's Pamela,' said a voice and my heart sank. 'Becky just rang and told me about Zoe's escapade. Silly girl! What on earth was she thinking? Threatening suicide is certainly not something that looks good on a parenting assessment.'

'She didn't actually threaten anything,' I told her. 'She didn't seem herself and I didn't want to take any chances. I think things had got on top of her and she said that she couldn't see a way out.'

'So you're saying it might all have been a false alarm?' she asked. I could hear the annoyance in her voice as if I'd been wasting her time.

'I really hope it was,' I told her. 'Alarm bells were ringing with the things she was saying and I didn't want to take that risk.'

I explained that when I'd seen her at contact the other night, she'd been upset about the message from the police saying that they were charging her with child endangerment.

'The thought of going to court was playing on her mind and she was worried about going to prison,' I told Pamela. 'I think it was a big shock.'

'I don't know why because we informed her at the LAC review that that was likely to happen,' tutted Pamela.

'Being warned but then knowing it's a reality is an entirely different thing,' I told her. 'I think everything that has happened in the past few weeks just came to a head.'

'Well, I'll need to speak to my manager about this,' sighed Pamela. 'All of this drama doesn't look good or help her case in any way.'

By the time I put the phone down, my upset had been replaced by frustration.

'That woman!' I said. 'Every time I speak to her, she just gets my back up.'

'It's really tricky when you're working with a social worker you really don't get along with,' nodded Vicky.

I looked at the time.

'You go if you want,' I told Vicky. 'Don't feel obliged to stay. I need to do some tidying up and get Lola some lunch so I'll make sure that I keep myself busy.'

'I'm not going anywhere until we know what's happened to Zoe,' she told me.

'Thank you,' I said gratefully.

I went to check on Lola and as I walked back into the kitchen, Vicky's mobile rang. We both looked at each other in panic and she pounced on it.

'Hello?' she said. 'Yes. I'll pass you over to her.'

As she handed me the phone, I realised that my hands were shaking.

A man introduced himself as the patient liaison worker at the local hospital.

'I'm calling you about Zoe,' he told me.

'Please tell me she's all right?' I asked, my heart pounding out of my chest.

'Yes, she's doing OK,' he replied. 'The paramedics found her at the top of the multi-storey and brought her here to be checked over and she's been admitted voluntarily for a psychiatric assessment.'

'So she's safe?' I gasped.

'She's fine,' he told me. 'A little shaken up but she's being well looked after.'

'Thank you so much for letting me know,' I said.

He gave me the ward details and I quickly wrote them down.

As I hung up the phone, relief flooded through me.

'She's OK,' I told Vicky.

'Thank goodness for that,' she nodded.

I quickly sent Becky a text to let her know that Zoe was safe in hospital.

What a relief, she replied.

It had been the most surreal morning but all I could do was carry on as normal. I wasn't going to tell the girls anything about what had happened with their mum and they didn't need to know she was in hospital. Their next contact session wasn't for a few days so we'd see where we were then.

I couldn't get Zoe out of my mind though. I knew from our chat the other day that she had no family around her and she struck me as someone who didn't have much of a support network, if any.

Later that afternoon when Vicky had gone and I'd picked Coco up from school, I gave Becky another call.

'I wanted to see if you thought it would be OK for me to go up to the hospital tomorrow to visit Zoe?' I asked her.

Becky hesitated.

'Maggie, you know your responsibilities are towards the girls and not the birth parent,' she told me. 'I'm worried that you're getting too involved here.'

'I know it's not normally the done thing but for my own peace of mind, I really need to see her and make sure that she's OK,' I told her. 'After everything that happened this morning, I feel like I need that closure.'

'I understand,' she told me. 'Under the circumstances, I think we can make an exception. What about the girls?'

'Coco will be at school and Louisa has said she'll have Lola for a couple of hours,' I told her.

I was so glad that Becky was happy for me to go and visit Zoe, but that night I hardly slept a wink. I kept replaying the events of that morning round and round in my head, wondering what I should have said or done differently.

The next morning, I dropped Coco off at school and then headed home with Lola.

'Louisa and Edie are coming round this morning,' I told her. 'They're going to look after you because I have to pop out for a little while. Is that OK?

Lola nodded.

'I can play with Edie,' she smiled.

'You can,' I told her. 'Edie loves playing with you because you're a big girl.'

I got a little wash bag that I already had at home and filled it with a new hairbrush, toothbrush and toothpaste, a mini shower gel, a flannel and some cleansing wipes. I assumed Zoe wouldn't have anything with her and it was always nice to have some essentials of your own when you were in hospital. I also printed out a couple of the photos of her with Coco and Lola that I'd taken when she was with them at my house to remind her of how important she was to them.

As I pulled up into the car park, I had flashbacks of rushing Lola here not so long ago. It felt like so much had happened in such a short space of time.

I walked through the hospital until I found the ward where Zoe was. A nurse pointed out her bed, which had the curtains pulled around it.

'Hello,' I called softly, as I pulled them back a chink.

Zoe was asleep in bed in a hospital gown. Her eyes fluttered when she heard me and she opened them.

'Hi, Maggie,' she croaked groggily.

'Hello,' I said gently. 'I wanted to come and see how you were doing.'

'Sorry, I was just dozing,' she said, trying to sit herself up.

'Doze away if you want,' I smiled. 'Don't mind me.'

Zoe seemed more frail than ever. Her eyes were puffy and swollen and she looked absolutely exhausted.

'Sorry, I must look a right state,' she said weakly, smoothing her hair down.

'That doesn't matter,' I replied. 'How are you feeling?'

'Tired,' she shrugged. 'Drained. Embarrassed. Ashamed.'

'Have you managed to get some sleep?' I asked her and she nodded.

'They gave me some pills to knock me out.'

She started to get tearful.

'I'm so sorry, Maggie,' she sobbed. 'I didn't mean to drag you into this mess. Thank you for everything that you did yesterday.'

'It's OK,' I soothed. 'I'm just glad you're fine. I was so worried about you. What on earth happened though? What were you thinking?'

She turned her head away from me and sobbed.

'I wasn't thinking,' she wept. 'I thought I'd be doing everyone a favour if I put an end to this mess.'

'But what about your girls?' I asked her. 'They need you.'

'Maggie, I meant what I said yesterday,' she wept. 'They deserve a better life than the one I can give them.'

'They want you,' I urged her. 'They love you.'

'And I love them,' she sobbed. 'With all my heart. I can't imagine life without them. They're my world, Maggie, but I've let them down. Lola could have died. I should never have left them that night.'

'You were doing the best you could,' I told her. 'It was a poor decision but it came from a place of desperation because you felt you had no other option.'

'No,' she said, shaking her head. 'I'm a bad mum. I neglected them, just like the police said, just like Pamela said and just like the judge at court will say. I don't deserve them. I know I need to let them go so they can move on with their lives with someone else.'

'They want you,' I repeated. 'They love you.'

'But love doesn't pay the bills,' she replied, wiping her eyes. 'Love doesn't pay the rent or a supermarket shop or being able to buy them decent clothes and wash in hot water and sleep in a warm, cosy bed.'

'You were in an impossible situation,' I told her. 'You felt there was no way out.'

'There's still no way out,' she said. 'I feel like I'm drowning. I can't keep my head above water. I don't deserve to be a mum.'

'There are things people can do to help,' I told her. 'Support they can give you and the girls.'

But Zoe seemed really despondent.

'I wasn't thinking straight yesterday,' she said. 'I hadn't slept in days and everything felt overwhelming. I promise you I'm not going to hurt myself but I have decided that if I am a good mum, I need to let the girls go.'

'You need to keep going for the girls,' I told her firmly. 'The hospital will refer you to a mental health worker and they can give you help and support. And you've got to keep going with your parenting assessment.'

Her face crumbled.

'There's no point now,' she sighed. 'I've completely ruined my chances of ever getting the girls back. Pamela came in this morning and told me that.'

'Told you what?' I gasped.

'She said that my parenting assessment probably couldn't continue because I've clearly got mental health issues and I was threatening to hurt myself so I wasn't putting the needs of the girls first.'

'What?' I gasped, anger rising up inside me. 'That's ridiculous.'

'She said the girls are probably going to get adopted now,' Zoe said. 'I just can't bear to even think about it, Maggie. I've messed everything up but I can't stand in their way. Coco and Lola deserve to have a good life and if I love them then I have to let them go.'

I was horrified by what I was hearing.

'Zoe, you need to fight this,' I told her. 'If you want your kids back and if you think what she's said is wrong, then you need to fight back.'

'I can't,' she sighed. 'I wouldn't know where to start. I haven't got the strength.'

'You have and you will,' I told her. 'This isn't fair or right.'

Zoe had a battle on her hands. I just hoped that she had the strength to fight it every step of the way.

CHAPTER 16

Speaking the Truth

Travelling home, all I could think about was what Pamela had said to Zoe. I couldn't understand why she would upset Zoe any further, especially in her current very fragile state of mind.

What Pamela had failed to disclose to Zoe was that it wasn't solely her decision. It wasn't only her who decided what happened to the girls, it was a collective decision made by everyone involved in their care. However, it had caused an already fearful Zoe to feel even more frightened about what the future held.

The girls were due to have a session at the contact centre the following day; however, I knew Zoe was unlikely to be there. I wasn't sure when she was going to be discharged but the doctors had said they wanted her to have at least a couple of nights in hospital and I wanted to prepare the girls for the fact that the next session probably wouldn't happen.

I chatted to them in the car on the way home from picking Coco up from school.

'I spoke to Pamela today,' I told them. 'And unfortunately Mummy won't be able to come to the next contact session because she's a bit poorly.'

I looked in the rear-view mirror but neither girl showed any reaction.

'I was poorly, wasn't I?' said Lola.

'Yes, you were, lovey,' I smiled. 'But you're feeling better now, aren't you? And hopefully Mummy will be better soon. Pamela will keep us updated and she'll arrange for you to see Mummy as soon as she's feeling well.'

'Why doesn't that lady like Mummy?' Coco asked suddenly.

'Which lady?' I asked. 'Pamela?'

Coco nodded.

'What makes you say that, flower?' I asked her.

'She's always asking us to tell her bad things about Mummy even when I say nice things,' sighed Coco.

The very essence of a social worker's role was to be non-judgemental and not have a fixed mindset. That had always been my worry about Pamela and now for Coco to notice it too, it was the final straw. I knew I had to speak out and voice my concerns to my supervising social worker. Parents could make a formal complaint about a social worker and they often did, but it was a lot trickier when you were a foster carer. Most carers felt that if they made an official complaint, they would be seen by Social Services as difficult to work with. I also knew from experience that it made your ongoing working relationship very difficult. I had complained about a social worker in the past and from then on, she made constant criticisms of my care whereas she hadn't done before. That was what Becky was there for – she was the buffer between me and Social Services, and she could have those difficult conversations on my behalf.

When we got home, I made the girls a snack and while they were playing in the kitchen, I went into the front room and rang Becky.

'I know I've mentioned this to you before, but my concerns are growing about Pamela. Even the children are picking up on it now.'

I went on to tell Becky about Coco's comments.

'I thought it might get better but Pamela only thinks in black and white,' I continued. 'Remember when the girls first came into care I told you that she was already talking about adoption?'

I then told her what Pamela had said to Zoe at the hospital.

'When someone's vulnerable like that in hospital, you don't go and tell them they're not likely to continue with their parenting assessment because of their mental health problems. Also, as you and I know, it's completely untrue.'

'It does seem unnecessarily harsh,' agreed Becky.

'My worry in all of this is, no matter what Zoe does, Pamela refuses to give her a chance. She made her mind up on day one and she won't budge from that, regardless of what happens with the parenting assessment.'

'Let me talk to my manager about it,' Becky told me. 'She might want me to contact Pamela's manager.'

'It would be worth getting the IRO's point of view from Heidi as well,' I suggested. 'She looked really exasperated with Pamela at the LAC review.'

It was difficult, even for Becky, to speak out against a social worker. You were criticising a professional so you had to go about it the right way. I knew Becky would do it as delicately as possible and work out how she and the agency could address my concerns.

'I don't feel like Zoe has a chance at all if Pamela is the girls' social worker and that really isn't fair,' I sighed.

'Thank you for speaking up,' said Becky. 'Leave it with me.'

Things escalated quickly. The next morning, I got a phone call from a woman called Moira at Social Services. She explained that she was Pamela's manager.

'Maggie, I wanted to talk to you about Pamela and how you find working with her,' she asked me. 'I know you've had a discussion with your supervising social worker about some of your concerns and I wanted to speak directly to you about it. Are you able to share your thoughts with me?'

I paused.

'Can I be completely open with you?' I asked.

'Of course, Maggie,' she replied. 'That's exactly what I want you to do. I want you to speak freely.'

There was no point in holding back now.

'I think Pamela has come into this case with a fixed mindset that the girls need to be adopted and I don't feel that Zoe stands a chance,' I told her.

'I can see for myself how Coco and Lola are with Zoe,' I added. 'When she's around, they light up. I can see the affection and love between the three of them and I believe that it's absolutely genuine. Pamela refuses to see any of that and in fact, completely disregards it.'

I explained that I thought Pamela seemed unable to get past the fact that Zoe had left the children at home alone.

'It's not that I believe Zoe shouldn't be held accountable for what she did,' I told her. 'She acknowledges that leaving the girls on their own at night was wrong but I don't feel that Pamela is looking at the "why".'

I explained that Zoe had no support network around her and felt like she'd had no other option at the time.

'Zoe has always put the girls first. She's gone without food herself to feed them, she's made sure Coco has always been in school and she had to work to be able to keep a roof over their heads. They might not have much materially but the girls feel loved and love in return. They've got good manners and have been taught personal care. They're not neglected children in that sense.'

'So what do you feel needs to happen?' asked Moira.

'Instead of taking her children away, I think we should be looking at how we can help and support Zoe to make sure that this situation doesn't arise again.'

I pointed out that even Coco had picked up on Pamela's negativity towards her mum.

'I'm sorry if I've said too much,' I told her.

'Not at all,' Moira replied. 'It's obviously something that you feel strongly about and I appreciate you being honest with me.'

When I'd hung up, I felt sick with worry. Had I done the right thing in speaking out? I knew social workers had a difficult job and were often juggling multiple cases so I wouldn't criticise anyone lightly. But on this occasion, I felt very strongly about Pamela.

I tried to forget about it and get on with my day but it was always there, niggling at the back of my mind. That afternoon I got a text from Zoe: *I've been discharged. Got antidepressants and sleeping tablets and back at the flat. OK for contact later in the week. Big kiss to the girls from Mummy x*

I was so relieved to hear that.

Really pleased. I hope you're feeling better, I replied.

The following morning, I was putting some clean dishes away in the cupboard when Becky rang me.

'I've just had an interesting call from Moira, Pamela's manager at Social Services,' she told me. 'Are you sitting down?'

'What do you mean?' I asked, pausing what I was doing.

'Pamela has been removed from the case.'

'What?' I gasped. 'Are you kidding me?'

'Not at all,' replied Becky. 'As of now, she's no longer Coco and Lola's social worker.'

I was in shock. Even though I had spoken out about my worries, I wasn't convinced Social Services were going to take them sufficiently seriously.

'Blimey, that all happened very quickly!' I said.

'Moira said she'd had concerns from a number of people so she felt this was the only option moving forwards.'

I felt a little bit guilty, but mainly just a huge sense of relief. It was the right decision and it meant that perhaps Zoe actually stood a chance now.

'What will happen now?' I asked.

'A new social worker is being appointed ASAP and you should be hearing from them today,' Becky told me.

I didn't have to wait long. An hour later I got an email from a woman called Danielle, who said she was Pamela's replacement: *I'd love to meet the girls, so please let me know if it's OK to pop round later when Coco is back from school.*

Absolutely, I replied. *Look forward to meeting you then.*

I knew I needed to tell the girls, so I casually mentioned it when we got home. Neither of them had particularly warmed to Pamela so I knew there would be no upset on their part.

'A lady called Danielle is going to call round and see us later,' I told them. 'She's your new social worker and she's really excited to meet you.'

Coco looked confused.

'But where's that other lady gone?' she asked.

'Oh, Pamela's really busy helping some other people at the moment,' I told her.

When Danielle arrived, she couldn't have been any more different from her predecessor. She was young – I guessed that she wasn't any older than twenty-five – and she wore jeans and trainers with a bright stripy jumper and had lots of piercings.

'You must be Coco and Lola,' she grinned in a loud, booming voice. 'I'm Danielle but you can call me Danny.'

As soon as she saw the girls, she got down on the kitchen floor and started playing with them.

I could see the girls eyeing her up suspiciously as if to say, 'Who is this?'

When Danielle went to the loo, I had a chat to them.

'Danny seems a nice lady, doesn't she?' I smiled.

'Better than the last one,' nodded Coco.

'She didn't play with us,' added Lola.

After Danielle had had a chat and a play with Coco and Lola, I made her a coffee.

'What gorgeous girls,' she smiled. 'So sweet and well-mannered.'

'They really are,' I nodded.

It was so nice to hear her acknowledging that.

'Maggie, I know there's been a few issues and concerns with

this case,' she told me. 'I'm yet to meet Zoe but I will and I've read all the files and reports and I want to reassure you that to me, this job is all about reuniting families wherever possible. I know that's not going to happen in every case and I'm afraid I can't give you any guarantees. I'm aware that Zoe has to go to court soon, so we need to wait and see what the outcome of that is, as well as the parenting assessment.'

'Absolutely,' I nodded. 'I'm just happy that you're coming to this case with an open mind.'

'You seem very positive about Zoe's relationship with the girls,' she said.

'I really am,' I told her. 'I understand that what Zoe did was wrong but it was more about circumstances and I believe she was coming from a place where she just wanted to do the best for her kids.'

I felt confident that Danielle was going to be looking at the whole situation and how Zoe got there, rather than just brand her a 'bad mother' because she had left her children.

It wasn't my place to tell Zoe the news about Pamela but someone clearly had as she left me a voicemail.

'Maggie, I can't believe it about Pamela. The new social worker has just left a message on my phone and she sounds really nice.'

For the first time, Zoe sounded positive and I felt that things were finally moving forward at last.

The next time I saw Zoe was at contact at my house a few days later. It was the first time that I'd seen her since she'd been in hospital and she still looked very fragile and shaky.

'How are you feeling?' I asked her and Zoe shrugged.

'OK,' she sighed. 'I'm sleeping a bit better thanks to the tablets but I still feel sad and anxious. I don't think I'll ever truly feel OK until I've been to court and I know I can get my girls back.'

'I know,' I nodded. 'But that's going to be a long way off, Zoe, and there are no guarantees.'

Zoe nodded, then she looked embarrassed. 'I know I didn't say it the other day as my head was all over the place but I just wanted to say thank you,' she told me.

I could see she was quite tearful.

'That's OK,' I told her. 'I could hear the pain and distress you were in and I would never want anything to happen to you.'

She nodded then reached into the pocket of her tatty jacket.

'I couldn't afford real flowers but I wanted to give you this,' she said.

She handed me a card. On the front in black pen was a simple drawing of a bunch of flowers and inside was a message.

Thank you, Maggie, for being there for me
when no one else was xx.

'Did you draw this?' I asked her and she nodded. 'It's really lovely, thank you.'

'You're the only one who doesn't think I'm a bad mum,' she told me.

'That's not true,' I replied.

We talked about the new social worker.

'What did you think of Danielle?' I asked her.

'I thought she was nice,' she nodded. 'She came round and had a chat with me and I felt like she was actually listening to me and what I was saying.'

'That's great,' I smiled. 'The girls really seem to like her too. It's a fresh start for all of you.'

Zoe looked down at the floor and started fiddling with her fingers.

'There was something I wanted to ask you, Maggie,' she told me.

She couldn't make eye contact with me and seemed nervous.

'I got a letter from the court,' she said. 'I have to go there next week for a plea hearing. My solicitor says that's when I have to say whether I'm guilty or not.'

'Do you know what you're going to say?' I asked her.

'I'm going to say I'm guilty,' she shrugged. 'The truth is, I am. I left the girls alone. My solicitor says I'll be able to tell them why, but I'm so scared, Maggie.'

Tears rolled down her cheeks.

'Nothing will happen at a plea hearing,' I told her. 'If you plead guilty then you'll have a sentencing hearing and that's when a judge will decide what's going to happen to you.'

'I know,' she nodded. 'I'm just so frightened about being in the court. So I was wondering . . . would you be able to come with me? I know it's a lot to ask but I'd love to have you there for moral support.'

My heart sank. I would have loved to have been there to support Zoe, but I knew that I couldn't.

'Zoe, I'm so sorry but while the girls are in my care, I'm not allowed to.'

'Please,' she begged tearfully. 'I don't want to be on my own.'

'I really wish that I could, but I can't,' I told her. 'I've got to be seen as being neutral.'

In reality, my role was to be there for the girls and be their advocate, and not Zoe's. Her children were still in my care so it might be seen as a conflict of interest.

'When's the hearing?' I asked her.

When she told me the date and time, I realised something.

'You're due to come here for a contact session that afternoon after the court hearing,' I told her. 'Why don't you come here a little bit earlier than normal after the hearing and you, me and Lola can go and collect Coco from school together and we can have a chat beforehand.'

'Yes, I'd like that,' she nodded. 'It will give me something to focus on.'

I couldn't be there for Zoe in court but I could be there for her afterwards and talk things through if she needed to.

'What am I even going to wear? Do you have to look posh?'

I looked at her worn, scruffy jeans and holey jumper.

'Not posh but it's good to look smart and give a good impression to the judge,' I said.

I could see the despair in her face and I knew she didn't have the money for new clothes.

'I tell you what,' I said. 'I've got some things that Louisa gave me a few months ago. Louisa is way slimmer than me so they're just gathering dust in my wardrobe. I'm sure there's a smart black jacket and some trousers up there. Why don't you take them home with you? They might be a bit big but it's worth a try?'

Zoe gave me a weak smile.

'Thank you,' she said gratefully.

She was still so frail, both mentally and physically. With the parenting assessment and the court case, the pressure was mounting and I hoped that Zoe had the strength she needed to get through the stress of the coming months.

SEVENTEEN

Becoming Mum

There was a knock at the door and I ran to answer it.

Zoe was standing there in Louisa's suit. The black jacket swamped her tiny frame and the trousers reached the ground, but I was glad that she had made the effort. She looked shell-shocked.

'Come on in,' I told her. 'How did it go at court?'

'It was really scary, Maggie. I was so frightened, I was shaking all the way through.'

I made her a cup of tea while she gave Lola a cuddle. When Lola went off to play, we were able to have a chat.

I could see that Zoe was relieved it was over but she was exhausted.

'It was scary but all I had to do was stand there and this man in a black gown read out what I'd been charged with, then I had to say I was pleading guilty.'

'That would have been the court clerk,' I nodded.

'I wished they could have told me there and then what was going to happen to me,' she sighed. 'But my solicitor said it's probably going to be a few weeks until the sentencing hearing.

'It's the waiting and the not knowing that's so hard,' she added. 'I can't think about the future. I don't know if I should be preparing the girls for the fact that I've got to go to prison or start packing the flat up.'

'All you can do now is focus on your parenting assessment and deal with it as it comes,' I told her. 'They need time to do a pre-sentencing report, which is really important.'

Zoe would be seen by a psychiatrist and she would have an interview with a probation officer, who would talk to her about her background and the girls in a bid to give the court some understanding of why she committed the offence.

'But what if I say the wrong thing?' Zoe asked.

'Just be honest with them,' I told her. 'It's important for you to talk about your mental health and the circumstances that led to you leaving the girls alone and how you felt you had no other option.'

'What if they think that makes me a bad mum like Pamela thought?' she asked.

'No one thinks that,' I told her. 'Pamela has gone now and anybody will understand how desperate you were at that point and how alone you must have felt.'

A pre-sentencing report would suggest the most appropriate sentence for the offence. The judge didn't have to take its recommendations but it was a helpful starting point for them.

'Will I get to read what it says about me?' asked Zoe.

'I think your solicitor will get a copy before the sentencing hearing so you can go through it with them and you can raise anything that you disagree with,' I told her.

'My head's spinning and I'm so tired,' sighed Zoe.

'I know, flower,' I told her. 'It's a lot to take in.'

She also had the parenting assessment sessions to get through and I knew that must have been adding to the pressure. These meetings covered all sorts of things, from money management to cooking nutritious foods to talking about Zoe's own childhood and experience of parenting. That was on top of her sessions with the girls where workers would observe her relationship with them and write up reports.

'How are you finding it all?' I asked Zoe.

'Intense,' she said. 'There's a lot to think about.'

She told me about a recent session where a support worker had asked her to describe what she would cook as a meal for the girls.

'She was talking to me about managing money and what I would spend it on when I went shopping at the supermarket,' she said. 'I wanted to shake her and say I know all about healthy food and I'd love to buy that for my girls, but where is this imaginary money coming from? That's how I've ended up in this mess, I hardly had any money to live on,' she shrugged. 'That's where I need the help, not talking about fruit and veg.'

I talked to her about booking an appointment with Citizens Advice.

'I think it would be good for you to check that you're claiming everything that you're entitled to,' I suggested.

'I want to work but I'm not able to work at the moment, what with court, Social Services and being in hospital,' Zoe sighed.

'You've got enough on your plate for now focusing on the parenting assessment,' I told her.

All I could think about was Zoe's fears when she had been standing at the top of that car park. In her head she still wasn't good enough for the girls and she didn't deserve them. I knew she needed to change her mindset if she was going to get through the parenting assessment and pass it. We needed to help build up her confidence to prove to herself and Social Services that she was more than good enough to be Coco and Lola's mum.

I knew that now we had Danielle as the girls' social worker, she might be a bit more open-minded about the different things we could do with the contact sessions.

One afternoon, I gave her a call.

'I wanted to have a chat to you about the contact sessions Zoe does at my house,' I told her. 'Do I always have to be in the room with her? Sometimes I feel like a spare part standing there watching her and I'd love her to be able to take the girls up for a bath on her own or put them to bed,' I added. 'I think Zoe would really like that too.'

'What have you been told to do in the past?' asked Danielle.

'Pamela told me I was to remain in the same room as her and the girls at all times and I wasn't to leave girls unsupervised with her.'

'How do you feel about it?' she questioned.

'I honestly don't feel Zoe is any threat to the girls,' I told her. 'She never has been. She's not at risk of hurting the girls or taking them. I don't have any worries about leaving her on her own in the same room as them and I would always be in the house. We've done a month of contacts with no problems at all,' I added.

'Well, I don't see a problem with it,' replied Danielle.

*

At the next contact session, I was washing up after dinner.

'Zoe, would you mind making a start on the girls' bath while I finish this?' I asked her.

She looked surprised.

'Yes, of course,' she said, obviously unsure. 'But are you sure that's allowed?'

'It's OK,' I nodded. 'Don't worry, I checked with Danielle and she hasn't got a problem with it.'

'Thank you so much,' she told me and I could see she was tearing up.

'Girls, you can go up with Mummy now,' I told them.

Zoe looked so happy as she walked out of the kitchen. It was just a small thing but I could see it meant so much to her to have time alone with her daughters, without me always lurking in the background. It took some of the pressure away and made it feel more normal.

After I'd finished clearing up, I went upstairs to check on Amena, who had just come home from a friend's house. As I wandered across the landing, I stood still for a minute and listened. I could hear the girls splashing and Zoe was telling them a story about mermaids and whales, which the girls were giggling at. I loved hearing their chatter and their genuine laughter and it made me smile. It was exactly as bath-time should be – happy, relaxed and fun.

After I'd talked to Amena for a while, I came out of her bedroom and Zoe was on the landing with the girls.

'All done,' she said proudly. 'They're in their PJs and ready for bed.'

'Brilliant,' I smiled. 'Well, let's pop them into bed then.'

I wanted to increase things gradually so at the next contact, I would let Zoe do bath and then put the girls to bed on her own.

'Would you like to stay for a quick cuppa?' I asked her as we wandered downstairs.

'That would be nice,' she nodded.

As I handed her a tea, she smiled.

'Thanks again for letting me do that,' she told me. 'I can't remember the last time I was allowed to be on my own with them. It was so lovely being with my girls and laughing and having fun.'

'It sounded like they were enjoying it too,' I smiled.

I could see it was like a weight had lifted off Zoe's shoulders – a moment of light relief amidst the stress and worry of the past few months.

Our chat invariably turned to the court case again and what potentially might happen.

'I can't bear to even think about it,' sighed Zoe.

She looked up at me, her green eyes, identical to the girls', filled with worry.

'If I did go to prison, would Coco and Lola stay with you?' she asked.

'I hope so,' I nodded. 'If Social Services let me, then I would be happy to keep them with me.'

'I'd really like that,' she told me. 'It would help me to know they were safe with you and then I wouldn't worry.'

But I could see she was absolutely terrified.

'I know you're scared,' I told her. 'But whatever happens, you'll get through it.'

'I'm preparing for the worst,' she almost whispered. 'My solicitor has said as much. He thinks a custodial sentence is likely.'

I reiterated again that Social Services would arrange for the girls to visit her even if she was in prison.

'I couldn't bear it for them to see me like that or to even know what prison is,' she sighed. 'I think it would traumatise them.'

'A lot of prisons have special contact rooms so you could see the girls there and not in the main visiting room,' I reassured her. 'It's not like you see on the TV and I doubt you would be in a high-security unit.'

'To be honest, Maggie, it makes me sick even thinking about it,' Zoe said.

Everything was hanging in the balance.

While Zoe was in turmoil, the girls were slowly getting used to the routine. They knew now they would see Mummy two or three times a week at the contact centre and at my house. I could see they were still processing things in their heads though.

After one contact visit when Zoe had put them to bed, I went upstairs to put some clean towels in the bathroom. Zoe had left about half an hour ago and I quietly popped my head around the girls' bedroom door to check on them. In the glow of the little night light, I could see that Coco's eyes were wide open.

'What are you doing still awake, lovey?' I whispered. 'You're going to be really tired at school tomorrow.'

'Are we going to live with our mummy ever again?' she asked.

I could see that she must have been lying there, going through everything in her little head.

'Well, Mummy and Danny are trying really hard to sort things out,' I told her. 'And they're doing lots of talking.'

'They're always doing talking,' she sighed. 'Just like the other lady.'

It was so hard not being able to reassure her or give her a definite answer.

'I know your mummy wants nothing more in the world than for you and Lola to live with her again but Danny has to make sure everyone is safe and happy.'

'If we can't go to our house, can Mummy come here for a sleepover?' she asked hopefully.

'That would be fun wouldn't it? But I'm afraid I don't do adult sleepovers,' I told her. 'My job is to look after children.'

Coco looked frustrated and confused, and I didn't blame her. All of the adults were repeating the same things over and over again because nobody had any answers for her.

A few days later, I was emptying her school bag when I found a scrunched-up ball of paper in the bottom.

'What's this?' I asked, opening it up and smoothing it out.

'Doesn't matter,' said Coco.

It was an invitation to a Mother's Day assembly at school.

'Why didn't you show me this?' I asked her.

'Because I know my mummy can't come,' she sighed sadly.

I put the invite on the side and reminded myself to ask Danielle about it. It had completely slipped my mind that Mother's Day was coming up.

I gave Danielle a quick call and told her about the assembly.

'It's not on a contact day but I know it would mean a lot to Coco if Zoe was there,' I told her. 'I would go too and we'd take Lola.'

'Thanks for suggesting it,' she told me. 'I feel we should be encouraging Zoe to do these normal, everyday things.'

'Thinking about it, do you think we'd be able to ask Zoe if she wanted to come round to my house on Mother's Day itself?' I suggested. 'I think it would really help her mental health and remind her that she's still the most important person in the girls' lives.'

'I don't see why not,' replied Danielle.

On the morning of the Mother's Day assembly, Zoe got herself to my house bright and early so I could drive us all to school.

'Mummy!' yelled Lola, throwing herself into her arms.

She was delighted to have Zoe sitting in the back seat between herself and Coco, and Lola gripped onto Zoe's hand from her car seat.

As we walked up to the school, Zoe looked nervous.

'I haven't been here in so long,' she said. 'Do you think everyone knows that my kids have been taken away? I bet they're all looking at me, judging.'

'Nobody thinks that,' I told her as we took our seats in the hall. 'I've never said anything to anyone and I know Mrs Evans wouldn't have either.'

The children were all sitting on benches up on the stage and as the assembly started, Coco was very fidgety and I could tell that she was nervous.

The whole class sung a joyful song about spring and then a few children did some readings.

'Now Coco would like to read a poem,' announced Mrs Evans.

Zoe and I looked at each other in surprise.

'That's my big sister,' beamed Lola, sitting on Zoe's knee.

Coco looked terrified as she stood up. She was holding a piece of paper and I could see that her hands were shaking with nerves.

Mrs Evans put her arm around her and gave her a quiet word of encouragement.

'My Mummy,' Coco said in a quiet voice.

'Try and speak a little bit louder so everyone can hear you,' said Mrs Evans.

Coco cleared her throat.

'This is a poem I've wrote about my mummy,' she said, loudly and confidently.

Zoe looked transfixed as Coco began to read.

> *My mummy.*
> *She makes up stories for me that are funny.*
> *She is like honey.*
> *Warm and sweet.*
> *It hurts my tummy when I'm not with my mummy.*
> *My special mummy.*

By the time Coco had got to the final line, tears were streaming down Zoe's face. She clapped and whooped enthusiastically and Coco had a huge grin on her face.

For the rest of the assembly, I could see Zoe was in bits. After the last song, Coco came running over to us.

'Did you like my poem, Mummy?' she asked Zoe.

'I didn't just like it,' she smiled, hastily wiping away her tears. 'I absolutely loved it. I'm so proud of you and I love you so, so much.'

'Do you think I was brave, Mummy?' Coco asked.

'Yes, I think you were really brave to stand up there and read that beautiful poem in front of everybody.'

I could see Coco was very proud of herself for having done it and that Zoe was there to see it.

'Well done,' I told her. 'That was amazing.'

She'd also written out a copy of the poem and drawn flowers around it, which she gave to Zoe. I could see that Zoe was struggling not to cry again.

'Are you OK?' I asked her quietly.

'I can't help but think, am I going to be putting this up on the wall of my prison cell?' she said, her voice shaking.

'Let's not think like that,' I told her. 'Let's be positive.'

Lola had something she wanted to ask Zoe.

'Mummy, can you come round on Mother's Day?'

'Yes,' nodded Coco. 'Maggie says it's OK.'

I nodded.

'Thank you,' she smiled. 'I would absolutely love that.'

The girls spent the rest of the week planning all the surprises they had in store for Zoe that Sunday. They made cards and we baked a cake and spelt out 'Mum' in chocolate buttons on the top. We got some bunches of daffodils from the supermarket and put them in a vase and the girls painted tubes of pasta, which they threaded onto a string to make a necklace for Zoe.

On Sunday morning, Coco and Lola stood by the front window, waiting excitedly for her to arrive.

'Surprise!' yelled Lola when Zoe walked through the door. They both took her hand and dragged her to the kitchen where they showed her all her gifts.

'Oh my goodness, this is so lovely, girls!' she exclaimed.

Zoe looked overwhelmed and I could tell that she was on the brink of tears all morning. After we'd eaten the shepherd's pie I'd made for lunch, the girls went outside in the garden to play.

'I hope the last few days haven't been too much for you,' I told her. 'The girls wanted to make it really special for you.'

Zoe shook her head.

'No, it's been amazing. For the first time in months, I've felt like their proper mum again.'

Suddenly, she reached into her pocket and pulled out a piece of paper that she put on the kitchen table.

'What's that?' I asked.

'I got a letter from the court,' she told me. 'The sentencing hearing is in two weeks.'

'Oh, goodness. I bet that's been playing on your mind?'

She nodded.

'I knew the other day when we were at school, which is why I was so emotional. All I can think is: is today going to be my last Mother's Day with them? Will I be behind bars this time next year?'

'It must be so hard and worrying for you,' I told her.

I couldn't reassure Zoe because the truth was that none of us knew what the judge was going to decide. The pre-sentencing reports had all been done now. Zoe's fate rested in the court's hands.

EIGHTEEN

Judgement Day

Zoe's eyes were wide with fear.

'Please, Maggie,' she pleaded. 'I know I asked you before, but this time I'm begging you – please could you come to court with me?'

I felt so guilty for letting her down but nothing had changed since the last time she'd asked me.

'I'm so sorry,' I said with feeling. 'I would love to be there for you, Zoe, but hopefully you understand that it's just not something I'm allowed to do.'

Zoe looked desperate.

'What if I asked Danielle?' she suggested. 'If she agreed to it, then would it be OK?'

She actually had a good point.

'OK,' I nodded. 'Run it by Danielle and see how she feels about it. If she's asking me then it puts a totally different perspective on it. I don't want there to be any comeback – that'll be all I need to cover my back.'

'I completely understand,' nodded Zoe.

I'd been to court to support children many times before but never a birth parent.

A couple of days later, Danielle called me.

'I've got a favour to ask you, Maggie,' she said. 'And you're completely free to say no, but Zoe has asked me if you could go to court with her for the sentencing hearing. I know your priority is the girls but she's clearly suffering and her mental health is so frail at the moment.

'I know this isn't the norm,' she added. 'But I'm happy for you to do it if it gives her the support she needs to get through the hearing.'

Danielle explained that she had offered to go to court with her. 'But she said that she'd rather it be you who goes with her,' she told me. 'I know you have a good relationship with her and it was you that she turned to when she hit rock bottom a few weeks ago.'

'I really feel for Zoe and I'd be happy to go to court with her if she felt it would help,' I replied. 'But I want to check that it doesn't put me in a compromising position with anybody or might be seen as a conflict of interest?'

'Not at all,' replied Danielle. 'You have my word. I've noted in the files that Zoe's request has come through me and it wasn't your idea.'

'Please could you run it by my supervising social worker, Becky, too?' I asked. 'I need to know my agency are aware and OK with it.'

I wanted to be open and transparent so no one could accuse me of not acting professionally further down the line.

Becky rang me shortly afterwards and gave me her blessing.

'I know it's not the norm, Maggie, but if Social Services

are fine with it and you're happy to do it then you have my backing,' she told me. 'It's very kind of you to support Zoe like that.'

'To be honest, all I'll be doing is sitting in the public gallery,' I replied.

'What about the girls?' she asked.

'Coco will be at school and Louisa has offered to have Lola for me,' I told her. 'I don't think it will take long as it's just a sentencing hearing.'

'How's Zoe holding up?' asked Becky.

'Not great,' I replied. 'She's convinced that she's going to go to prison.'

Zoe was immensely relieved when I told her that I was going to be able to accompany her to court.

'Danielle and Becky have given me special permission,' I said.

'Oh, I'm so grateful,' she said with feeling. 'It really means a lot, thank you.'

I wanted things to go as smoothly as possible for her. I took up the hems on Louisa's old trousers for her and I offered to give her a lift to court on the morning of the hearing.

The next few days passed in the usual blur of contact sessions and getting Coco to school. But the shadow of the sentencing hearing was looming large in the background. Every time I saw Zoe she looked exhausted and I could tell that she wasn't sleeping well again.

'If you feel like you're not coping then you need to talk to your GP,' I urged her. 'They might be able to up your medication temporarily.'

'I'm OK,' she sighed. 'I just can't wait for it to be over.

In a strange way, even prison would be a relief after all this waiting. At least I'd know what I was doing.'

'You don't mean that,' I said.

By the time it was the morning of the hearing, I was also a bag of nerves.

'I don't know why I'm feeling so jittery,' I told Louisa. 'It's not me in the dock.'

I'd put a blouse and some navy trousers on.

'Gosh, you look smart,' said Louisa.

'Thanks,' I smiled. 'I thought I'd better make an effort.'

Even though I was only sat in the public gallery, there was something about going to court that made me nervous. I always felt better if I was dressed appropriately and I didn't want to look scruffy in jeans and a jumper.

I knew how much was resting on this day. We all knew that what happened in court would help determine whether Zoe got Coco and Lola back full-time or not. I felt more strongly than ever that Zoe didn't deserve to go to prison; I just hoped the judge saw that too.

I said goodbye to Lola, who was blissfully unaware of what her mummy was about to face, and got into the car to go and pick up Zoe.

As I pulled up outside the run-down block of flats, she was already waiting on the pavement outside. She looked ashen.

'How are you doing?' I asked her.

'Awful,' she replied. 'I've hardly slept.'

'It's going to be OK,' I soothed. 'At least it will all be over soon and you'll know what's happening.'

'Thank you for helping me with the trousers,' she said. 'And look what I've got in my pocket . . .'

She pulled out the pasta necklace that Coco and Lola had made her for Mother's Day.

'This way it feels like the girls are with me,' she told me. 'I feel I need all of the luck I can get this morning.'

The sentencing hearing was being held at the Crown Court, a place I'd been to several times in the past. It was a large modern building with a huge glass atrium. Once we'd passed through security and had our bags searched, Zoe saw her barrister waiting for her.

'Can you come with me?' she asked.

'I think you need to go with your barrister and I have to sit in the public gallery,' I told her. 'But I'll see you in the courtroom.'

She looked terrified.

'What's going to happen to me, Maggie?' she asked suddenly.

All I could do was give her a hug but I could feel her heart thumping out of her chest. She was getting more and more panicked.

'Remember to breathe,' I told her calmly. 'It's really important that you're calm and able to follow what's happening and listen to what the judge is saying. This will be over and done with soon.'

But Zoe was getting more and more wound up. 'But what if I go to prison?' she started ranting. 'What will happen to me and the girls? Does that mean I'll never get them back?'

She was getting hysterical now and I didn't want her to go into court like that.

'Whatever happens, you will get through it,' I told her.

'You've got lots of people who are here to support you and the girls.'

I put my hand on her arm.

'Good luck,' I told her. 'We'll work it out together.'

'Thank you,' she replied. 'I'm just so scared.'

Zoe looked like a rabbit caught in headlights as her barrister led her off into one of the waiting areas.

I must admit, I felt my own stomach fizzing with nerves as I pushed open the heavy door of Court Eight, where the hearing was being held.

It was one of the smaller courts and there were hardly any people in there as I took a seat in the public gallery. Two court clerks were having a chat but there was no one else around. As I sat there, I thought of Coco at school and Lola back at my house with Louisa. They'd already had so much change in their little lives and the idea of Danielle and I having to sit them down and tell them Mummy had gone to prison was unbearable.

The court soon began to fill up. Zoe's defence barrister, whom I'd seen earlier, and a man who I assumed was a prosecution barrister, walked in together, holding bundles of papers. The court clerks were still chatting and laughing. It was a normal working day for them; meanwhile Zoe's life hung in the balance.

Finally, Zoe was brought up into the dock that had clear Perspex sides. She looked terrified. When she looked around and saw me, I gave her what I hoped was a reassuring smile.

'All rise please,' said the clerk.

A hush descended over the court as the judge walked in and introduced himself. He was a stern-faced man in his fifties and, like most judges, wore a short grey wig and a long black gown.

Zoe looked like she was going to collapse and gripped the ledge in front of her.

Firstly, it was the prosecution barrister's turn to open the hearing and address the judge. He summarised the case and presented the facts to him. He described how Zoe had been arrested for shoplifting then the girls were found at home alone by the police and taken into care.

'As you know, Miss White has pleaded guilty to one count of child neglect but we believe this wasn't a one-off event. It's the only incident that we can prove but we would urge Your Honour to consider the fact that we think this was a regular occurrence. In fact, during questioning, the defendant admitted that she'd recently had a cleaning job working nights and she wasn't allowed to take her children with her.'

As he continued, Zoe bowed her head in shame.

'Around nine hours after being taken into the care system, one of her children – her three-year-old daughter – was rushed to hospital by her foster carer and treated for pneumonia. Not only had Miss White left two children at home alone, she had left a very sick child in a freezing cold flat with no heating or electricity.

'We would argue that Miss White is very lucky that her daughter was treated in time and that she's not appearing before the courts today on a manslaughter or even a murder charge as things could have been very different.'

As the prosecution barrister laid out all of the accusations for the judge, Zoe wept quietly in the dock.

It was all true but my heart broke for her and I wanted to

rush over and give her a hug.

Then it was the defence barrister's turn.

'When you are considering sentencing today, Your Honour, I would urge you to look at the "why". My client was a victim of circumstances – a young, single mother with no familial support trying to do her best for her daughters.

'She didn't want to survive on benefits but she struggled to find flexible work without being able to afford childcare. The only work she could find was in the evenings.

'Trapped in unsafe and unsuitable accommodation, my client was taken advantage of by an unscrupulous private landlord who kept increasing the rent, which meant my client was continually in debt. She struggled to pay all the bills and would often go without food herself to make sure that her daughters were fed.

'The night of the offence, she knew her daughter was unwell although she didn't realise how seriously. However, she knew she had no money for medication. In a fit of desperation, she knew the only way to get that for her daughter was to steal it.'

It was heartbreaking to hear Zoe's life laid bare like that.

The defence barrister continued.

'My client accepts that she has done wrong. She knows it was a terrible decision to leave her children at home alone but it was driven by complete and utter desperation. Miss White loves her children and, more than anything in the world, she wants them back. I appeal to the court not to opt for a custodial sentence today and allow her to try to win custody again of the two little girls who are desperately missing their mummy.'

Hearing her own barrister's words, Zoe was in floods of

tears. I could see how much distress she was in and tears started filling my eyes too.

Throughout all of this, the judge had been listening attentively and taking notes. Now it was his turn to address Zoe. He looked sternly at her over his wire-rimmed glasses.

'Miss White, as you know, it is a criminal offence to leave a child alone if it places them at risk or harm. Your daughters were of an age where they were much too young to be left alone regularly, particularly on the night of the offence, in view of your younger daughter's medical condition. As my learned colleague pointed out, it was fortuitous that her foster carer was able to seek urgent medical treatment otherwise you could be facing a very different charge in this court today.'

Zoe shook her head.

'I'm sorry,' she whispered. 'I'm so, so sorry. I'll never ever forgive myself for that.'

'From reading all of the reports from Social Services and the pre-sentencing documents, it is clear that you love your children, which is what makes it all the more baffling why you chose to knowingly put them at risk in that way.'

Zoe looked absolutely crushed. My palms were sweating and I felt sick. All of his comments seemed to be suggesting that he was going to give her a custodial sentence.

He paused.

'However, all of the reports that I have read paint you as a loving and capable mother.'

'I am,' nodded Zoe. 'I promise you, I really am.'

'You have no previous convictions and you are a person of previous good character. You've been very open and honest about your failings, you have admitted this offence and you understand the gravity and seriousness of leaving two young children alone at night. You clearly had a lack of support and found yourself in a difficult situation where you felt there was no way out.'

Zoe nodded.

'As your barrister has probably informed you, child neglect can carry a custodial sentence of up to ten years . . .'

Zoe slumped forward in the dock, preparing herself for the worst. I held my breath.

The judge paused.

'However, in this case, I do not believe that a custodial sentence would be in the best interests of your children. I know in recent months you have had to cope with your children being taken into care and unsurprisingly, your mental health has suffered as a result. On reflection, I feel like this is punishment enough. Therefore, I sentence you to a six-month community order.'

Thank goodness.

My body sagged with relief and I felt like I could finally breathe.

'A failure to comply with this order will lead you to appear back in this court where there will be no other choice than to impose a custodial sentence,' the judge told her. 'I hope that you're able to access more help and support and I wish you and your daughters the very best of luck for the future.

'You're now free to go.'

'All rise,' said the clerk.

With that, the judge got up and left.

Zoe stood in the dock, looking both stunned and confused.

'What does that mean?' she asked her barrister. 'Am I

going to prison?'

I walked over to her.

'Zoe, it's OK,' I told her. 'You heard the judge – you're free to go.'

'So I'm not going to prison?' she gasped.

'No,' I smiled.

'You'll have to do some sort of community service for the next six months, which will have to be worked out,' her barrister told her, 'but no, you're not going to go to prison.'

'I think I need to sit down,' Zoe said.

She stepped out of the dock and sat on the empty press bench. She put her head in her hands and wept. I sat down next to her and put my arm around her.

'I can't believe it! I was so convinced that that was it and I was going to be locked up.'

'I'm so pleased for you,' I told her. 'The judge could see what you'd been through.'

I felt like the court had made the right decision.

Her barrister got her a glass of water and slowly Zoe started to calm down.

'I'm so glad that's over,' she said. 'There's only one thing that I need to do now and that's get my girls back.'

She turned to me.

'Maggie, do you think I can do it? Do you think I've done enough to convince Social Services to give them back to me full-time?'

I honestly didn't know the answer to that one.

NINETEEN

Decision Time

When we finally left the court, I could see Zoe was still in shock.

'I feel like I could do with a brandy and I don't even drink!' she joked.

'I'm afraid you'll have to make do with a cup of sugary tea from the vending machine,' I smiled.

As she sat down on a bench in the atrium and sipped on a plastic cup of strong, sweet tea, I could see her visibly sag as the adrenalin left her body.

'How are you feeling?' I asked her.

'Relieved but very tired,' she replied. 'But it's not over yet. I have to do everything I can to get my girls back. That's the only thing that matters to me now. The judge believed I wasn't a bad mother, I just made some stupid decisions. Social Services have to believe that too.'

However, we both knew there was no guarantees.

'You've just got to do everything Social Services ask of you and to the best of your ability,' I told her.

'I know,' she nodded. 'I'm really trying.'

As she stood up and put her cup into the bin, we saw Danielle running over to us.

'I'm sorry I'm so late,' she puffed. 'I got held up at a meeting in town. How did it go?'

'I'm not going to prison,' Zoe told her.

'That *is* good news,' she smiled.

I explained what the judge had said and that Zoe had been sentenced to a six-month community order.

'Now that I'm not going to prison, can I get my girls back?' Zoe asked her.

'I'm afraid it's not as simple as that,' Danielle told her. 'You need to carry on with the last few weeks of the parenting assessment and we'll see how that goes. We have to make sure that everyone involved in the girls' care is in agreement about the best way to move forwards.'

So far, the feedback from Zoe's sessions had been good but she couldn't take anything for granted. Sadly, I'd seen parents fall apart in the last few weeks of a parenting assessment when the pressure got too much.

However, today had been a positive one for Zoe.

Over the next few weeks, Zoe was on tenterhooks. The court proceedings were over but she was having sleepless nights about the parenting assessment and what would happen at the end of it.

'I think I'm doing OK but no one knows what the final decision will be,' she told me.

But D-day was fast approaching. A few days after her assessment ended, another LAC review was scheduled at Social

Services. Heidi, the IRO, was chairing it and Danielle was there, as well as Mrs Evans, Becky and I.

Zoe knew how important this meeting was and how much was resting on it and she was tearful before it had even started.

As before, she sat down next to me at the large table.

'Are you OK?' I asked her. 'Your hands are shaking.'

'I feel sick,' she replied. 'This feels even worse than going to court because it directly involves the girls and whether I'm going to get them back or not.'

'It will be OK,' I told her. 'Whatever decision is made today, everyone is here to support you and Coco and Lola.'

'But are they?' she asked me and I could tell that she wasn't so sure.

Zoe knew that, despite what had happened at court, Social Services still had the power to say that she couldn't have the girls back full-time if they still had any doubts or concerns about her and her parenting.

'What if they decide that Coco and Lola can't live with me any more?' she sobbed. 'I couldn't bear it. I honestly don't know what I'd do.'

'Let's see what happens,' I told her. 'Everyone will give their view and you'll have a chance to speak.'

Once everyone was settled around the table, Heidi opened the meeting.

She turned first to Zoe.

'Gosh, you must feel so relieved about the court proceedings,' she told her.

'I really am,' nodded Zoe. 'It's nice not to have the threat of prison hanging over me and I feel like I can move on with my life now.'

'And, as we all know, the girls have got a new social worker,' said Heidi, gesturing over to Danielle.

Zoe nodded.

'How are things going?' Heidi asked.

'Absolutely brilliantly,' said Zoe. 'Danielle's really good with the girls and she's been so kind and understanding with me.'

'I know you've only been the girls' social worker for a short time, Danielle, but how do you feel it's going?' Heidi asked her.

'I've read all of the reports from the contact workers and, as you will have seen, they're glowing,' she told us. 'I've been able to observe Zoe with the girls at the contact sessions myself and I have to say, they have a lovely relationship and it doesn't give me any cause for concern.'

Zoe smiled.

Then Heidi turned to Mrs Evans to get an update about how Coco had been at school.

'Coco has been OK,' said Mrs Evans. 'She's always been a well-behaved and conscientious little girl and that hasn't changed.'

'Does she ever talk about her mum?' asked Heidi.

'She's told me how much she misses her and she wrote the most beautiful, heartfelt poem about her mummy, which she asked if she could read out at the assembly we had for parents.'

'That sounds lovely,' smiled Heidi. 'I bet there wasn't a dry eye in the house.'

'There wasn't,' sniffed Zoe tearfully. 'I was so proud of her. She and Lola have been so brave throughout all of this.'

I put my hand on hers to try to offer some comfort.

Then it was my turn to speak.

'Maggie, how have you found the placement?' Heidi asked me.

'It's been a bit of an unusual one for me,' I replied. 'Normally when I'm told neglected children are coming into my care, there are usually all sorts of issues around food, behaviour, hygiene and sleep.

'However, Coco and Lola have never presented like that. Understandably, they were scared and traumatised by coming into the care system but they had manners, they knew how to keep themselves clean, dress themselves and brush their teeth. They could use a knife and fork and sit nicely at the table. They could play on their own and with others and they were used to a routine and boundaries.

'From what they told me, I knew that they didn't have the most ideal living conditions and that their financial situation was precarious but emotionally, they weren't what I would class as neglected children. So this placement has been about keeping things stable for them and offering them reassurance.'

If anything, my unofficial role had been to support Zoe. I hoped that I'd helped her believe things could be different and that she was a good mum to her girls.

'What are your observations about Zoe?' Heidi asked me.

'I've got to know her quite well over these past few months,' I replied. 'And lately she's come round to my house to bathe the girls and put them to bed. Coco and Lola have missed her desperately and I can see the love they have for her by how relaxed and happy they are when she's around.'

'Do you have any concerns about the girls being in her care?' asked Heidi.

Under the table, I could feel Zoe nervously jiggling her leg next to me. I knew I had to be honest here.

'Zoe has had her ups and downs. She has struggled in the past and she admits herself that she made some bad decisions as a result. Her mental health has been affected by all of the worry and uncertainty, but I feel strongly that the girls are not at risk in her care. She's a good mother.'

Zoe looked up at me and smiled.

'Thank you,' she mouthed.

Zoe looked over at Heidi and put her hand up.

'I've listened to what everyone else has said, but please could I say something?' she asked timidly.

'Of course you can,' replied Heidi.

'I know that I've made mistakes,' she sighed. 'I made some stupid decisions and I put my girls at risk and for the rest of my life, I will never, ever forgive myself for that.'

She explained that at the time she'd felt like there was no way out.

'Everything was a struggle – finding work, finding enough money for rent, food and bills and most of the time, I didn't. I was desperate. But I've spent the past few months trying to make things right,' she added. 'I've tried really, really hard to prove that the girls are safe with me and I don't think I can do any more. I promise you, I *am* a good mum.'

I could hear the emotion in her voice and I felt my own eyes filling with tears.

'I love Coco and Lola so much – they are my absolute world. So I'm begging you, please let me have my girls back. Please let them come home to their mummy and give me a chance to make up for everything that I've done.'

After she'd finished her plea, Zoe burst into tears. I couldn't bear to see someone so upset so I put my hand on her arm and gave her a reassuring squeeze.

'I'm OK, Maggie,' she told me. 'I just needed to get that off my chest.'

'You're doing really well,' I replied.

Heidi got up to get Zoe a glass of water and put it down on the table in front of her.

'Thank you for that, Zoe,' she told her. 'Your love for your daughters really shines through in your words and also in all of the reports that I've read from your parenting assessment. However, I think it's important that we ask you some tough questions.'

Zoe looked up anxiously.

'How do we know that this won't happen again?' Heidi asked. 'How do we know you won't start to struggle again and the girls will be regularly left alone?'

'I promise you, my head is in a totally different place now,' Zoe told her. 'I have support around me and now I know that I don't have to struggle alone. Next time, I would ask someone for help instead of getting myself deeper and deeper into debt or feeling like things were out of my control and I couldn't cope.'

Heidi nodded and looked at her notes.

'Throughout this process, you've had a few wobbles though, haven't you?'

Zoe nodded tearfully.

'There have been a couple of times that it's all got too much for me,' she sobbed. 'But it was more about not coping with the fact that the girls had been taken into care and the worry about going to prison.

'Please,' she sobbed. 'I'm begging you. I just want my babies back.'

Zoe wept quietly while Heidi made a few more notes in her notebook.

'Thank you for being so honest, Zoe,' she nodded. 'I'm just trying to get an understanding of where your head is at.'

There was no one else left to speak now and all eyes were on Heidi.

'Before I bring the meeting to a close, I want to thank everybody for all of their feedback and Zoe for your commitment to the process,' she said. 'You've worked really hard and I'd like to thank you for your transparency and your honesty. I know things can't have been easy for you.'

Zoe nodded. All of the colour had drained from her face and she looked as if she might pass out.

She knew this was it. Decision time.

I felt my own stomach churning with nerves and anticipation.

'Reading the reports and talking to you all today, I'm pleased to say that it all sounds incredibly positive,' smiled Heidi. 'So I feel that the next part of the process is about looking at moving the girls back home.'

TWENTY

Home Is Where The Mummy Is

Zoe looked stunned.

'What do you mean?' she gasped. 'You mean I can have them back?'

'That's right,' nodded Heidi. 'I can see no reason why Coco and Lola can't move back in with you full-time. Danielle will still be around to offer help and support but our eventual goal is for the girls to leave the care system.'

'Zoe, I'll leave you in Danielle and Maggie's capable hands and you can work out a plan after this meeting,' she added.

I turned to Zoe, who looked stunned.

'Well done,' I smiled. 'You absolutely smashed it.'

'I– I don't know what to say,' she stuttered. 'I can't believe it.'

'Well, you'd better start believing it as two little girls will hopefully be moving back in with you soon,' said Danielle.

Even though Zoe was getting Coco and Lola back, we wouldn't go straight into overnight stays. Instead, we'd build things up gradually. Zoe hadn't had any great lengths of time on her own with the girls unsupervised and Social Services wanted to make sure everyone was comfortable and happy.

'Maggie, how would you feel about Zoe picking up the girls one day and taking them back to the flat for tea and you picking them up later?' Danielle suggested.

'That works fine for me,' I replied.

We also arranged for Zoe to pick them up at the weekend and take them back to the flat for the day.

'Then in the second week you could have them to stay overnight,' Danielle told her.

'But the flat's still a run-down mess,' Zoe said.

'Now we know that the girls will be returning to you, I'm sure Danielle would be able to write a letter of support to the housing department so that you're a priority and your GP might be able to write a letter too,' I suggested.

'Absolutely,' nodded Danielle. 'And in the meantime, Social Services will be able to fund some beds and bedding for the girls.'

'Thank you,' replied Zoe.

Danielle was also going to organise another meeting with Zoe so she could run through the full package of support that they would put in place for Zoe and the girls to make sure the same situation didn't happen again.

Now we had to break the good news to Coco and Lola.

'I'll come round and speak to them after school today,' Danielle told me.

She would deliberately talk to them without Zoe being there as she'd want to see their reaction and check that they were genuinely happy or if they had worries or concerns.

As I drove home that morning, it felt like a weight had

been lifted from my shoulders. For once we would be able to give the girls some really positive news and answer their questions. It was hard to keep it to myself as I walked in the front door and saw Lola.

'All OK?' asked Louisa.

'Yes,' I smiled. 'It went really well.'

Later that afternoon as we pulled in from collecting Coco from school, Danielle was already on the doorstep.

'I've come to talk to you two about something really important,' she told them.

I got them a drink and a biscuit each and we all sat around the kitchen table.

'Danielle has got some very exciting news to share with you,' I grinned.

'We had a meeting this morning and we all decided that you can both go back to live with Mummy.'

Coco and Lola looked at each other and smiled.

'Today?' asked Coco.

'Not today,' I told her. 'But we've come up with a special plan.'

We explained to them how it was going to work over the next two weeks.

'You're going to have tea with Mummy at your flat, then another time you'll spend the day there and then the next time you can do a sleepover,' I told them. 'And if that goes really well, you can do two sleepovers and after that you can move back to Mummy's flat.'

'For ever and ever?' asked Coco, and Danielle, and I nodded, smiling.

I could tell it would take them a few days to properly absorb the news but they were really excited and Danielle didn't have any concerns about the way they'd reacted.

The next few days passed in a blur of arrangements. Zoe came to pick the girls up the following day and they were going to get the bus back to her flat for tea. The girls ran round the house excitedly.

'Shall I get my pyjamas, Mummy?' Coca asked.

'You're coming for tea today, sweetheart, so you won't need them just yet,' Zoe told her.

'It's not forever yet, is it, Maggie?' she asked me, obviously trying to get it straight in her head.

'Not yet,' I smiled. 'But it will be after the next few weeks.'

The first couple of visits went really well. The girls were happy when they came back and I could see Zoe was savouring every minute.

'It's lovely having the flat noisy again,' she said. 'It's been so quiet without them.'

Zoe also told me about the meeting that she'd had with Danielle.

'It's amazing, Maggie,' she sighed.

Social Services were going to fund a nursery place for Lola three days a week so Zoe could work, and Coco now had a funded place at the breakfast club and after-school club at her primary school.

'There's even a support worker who can come round and go through my money with me if I feel like I'm struggling again,' Zoe told me. 'She checks I'm on all the right benefits and getting everything I'm entitled to and she can help me with my bills and budget.'

'That's wonderful,' I told her. 'Everyone wants you and

the girls to be happy and comfortable.'

She had also been given a list of voluntary organisations that she could contact if she needed emergency help, such as food or even clothes or uniforms for the girls.

'I never even knew these places existed,' she said.

'Often to access these things you have to have a referral by Social Services,' I explained.

I could see that she felt really supported.

At the weekend, the girls were having their first overnight stay with Zoe at the flat. I'd offered to drop Coco and Lola off as they would have their stuff with them. They helped me pack a bag for them and we put it in the car.

It was dark by the time I pulled up at the flat, which was in a large Victorian building. Zoe had already told me the buzzer was broken so she came down to let us in. The run-down entrance hall felt damp and cold and there was only one bare light bulb working. She took us up to the first floor.

'Here we are,' she told me, pushing open the front door. It didn't fit the frame properly and the wood was splintered and the paint was peeling off.

'It's nice and warm in here,' I said as we walked in.

'Danielle made sure the gas and electric meter were both topped up,' Zoe told me.

'I'll give you a tour,' she said. 'Starting with the worst bit. This is the girls' old bedroom,' she said, pushing open the door.

The room was damp and dank. The wallpaper was peeling off and there was black mould growing on the walls.

'I've scrubbed it and bleached it but there's just no getting it

223

off,' she sighed. 'I even tried to paint over it but it didn't work.'

'Gosh, what a state. It's disgusting that the landlord wouldn't do anything about this.'

'Don't worry, the girls won't be going anywhere near this room,' she told me. 'We're all going to have a sleepover in my room. Wait until you see this, girls,' she told them.

She took us into the other bedroom.

'We've got beds!' yelled Coco excitedly.

'Beds! Beds!' echoed Lola.

There were two single beds side by side with pink flowery duvets and pillows on them. The girls leapt on them and started bouncing around.

'It's just like at Maggie's house,' beamed Coco.

'Danielle's been brilliant,' Zoe told me. 'She managed to get us these, like she promised, and the duvets and all the bedding.'

'But what about you?' I asked her. 'Where are you going to sleep?'

'Oh, I'll be OK with some cushions on the floor,' she said. 'That's what I'm used to.'

I made a mental note to try to get hold of a bed from somewhere for her.

I was shocked at the state of the rest of the flat but I tried not to show it. I could see Zoe had done her best to make it homely and clean and it was warm now at least as the storage heaters were on. But the carpets were old and stained, the windows were cracked and badly fitted, letting in the cold, and the bathroom and the kitchen were run-down and dated. The whole place needed gutting and I couldn't believe they had lived like this for so long.

'Coco, I've got another surprise for you,' Zoe told her. 'Look,' she said, turning on the kitchen tap.

Coco stuck her hand underneath it and her face lit up.

'It's warm!' she yelled. 'We've got one like you, Maggie.'

'And the one in the bathroom is warm too,' Zoe told her. 'No more magic washes.'

I knew I needed to go and let the three of them have some time together. Before I left, I handed Zoe a couple of carrier bags filled with food. I didn't know how her finances were and I didn't want her and the girls to go hungry.

'I thought you might like these,' I told her. 'It's some cereal the girls like at the moment and I had loads of milk left so I've bunged you four pints in there as it will just go off at my house. There are a few other bits in there that I don't need.'

I'd put in some packets of biscuits, a loaf of bread, some eggs and a couple of cans of baked beans.

'Thank you, Maggie,' Zoe said. 'I really appreciate everyone rallying round me like this. I feel really looked after.'

'Have a lovely time with Mummy,' I told the girls who were both giggling and pretending to be asleep in their new beds.

As I drove home, I didn't have any doubts at all. Their flat might have been a state but in a way, that didn't matter. They were all together at last.

Zoe brought the girls back on the bus in the morning and they were full of chatter about their sleepover with Mummy.

'Would you like to do it again later this week?' I asked them. 'And this time you can have two sleepovers and Mummy will take you to school, Coco, and pick you up.'

Danielle called me.

'I've spoken to Zoe and she's happy but from your perspective, Maggie, how are things going?'

'It couldn't be better,' I said. 'Zoe seems to be coping well and the girls are happy and going to the flat without any hesitation.'

'That's amazing,' she replied. 'I think it's full steam ahead then for Coco and Lola to move permanently next weekend.'

'That sounds like a plan,' I smiled.

I didn't have big plans for Coco and Lola's last night with me. I wasn't one for huge goodbyes anyway. I didn't think it did me or the children any good to have a lingering farewell with lots of weeping and wailing. It wasn't going to be easy though; the girls were absolutely adorable, loving and so easy to love, and I knew I was going to miss them. However, I refused to let myself feel sad because I knew they were going back to where they belonged – to their mummy. I could also see how happy Zoe was. These past few days she'd been like a different person. All the worry and stress of the past few months had lifted. I knew she had to build her confidence back up and, after everything that had happened, it would take time, but I could see she was enjoying feeling like a proper mother again.

On their last night, Amena came home straight after school and I made us all bangers and mash and peas – the girls' favourite tea.

'You must be so excited about going to live with Mummy tomorrow,' I told them.

'But what about you?' Coco asked me sadly. 'What are you going to do?'

'I will miss you both very much but I've still got Amena living here so I'll be looking after her,' I told her.

'Will she go back and live with her mummy one day?' asked Coco.

Amena nodded.

'I hope so,' I smiled.

Lola was too young to really understand but I could tell that Coco was getting everything straight in her head. That night as I tucked her in for the last time, she gave me a hug.

'Maggie, has all the talking stopped now?' she asked. 'Is everyone safe?'

I couldn't help but smile. Poor kid, that's all I'd been telling her for the past few months.

'Yes, it has,' I said. 'Everyone has spoken to Mummy and they know what a great mummy she is and how happy you and Lola are going to be with her and that's why you're going home.'

Coco nodded.

The next morning, there was no time to be sad or dwell on anything. I ran round the house, packing the girls' things up. Even though they'd only been with me a few months, they'd managed to accumulate a lot of stuff. Eventually we'd packed it all into the car and were ready to go.

When we got to the flat, Zoe was already waiting outside for them. They waved and leapt into her arms.

When we'd brought everything in from the car, Zoe asked if I'd like to stay for a cup of tea.

'Just a quick one,' I smiled.

'I've had some good news,' she told me as she put the kettle on. 'We've been allocated a house.'

'That's brilliant,' I told her. 'I'm so happy for the three of you.'

She sounded so excited as she told me about it. It was a two-bedroom newbuild on a nice estate and a short bus ride away from Coco's school.

'Everything is brand new,' she told me excitedly. 'No mould, no damp and it's all painted and ready for us! Danielle said Social Services can help with some furniture and a fridge and a washing machine too.'

I was over the moon for her.

'These might come in useful then,' I told her, handing her a bag. 'I was having a big clear-out the other day and I realised I've got loads of spare bedding and towels that I just don't need. I wondered whether you might be interested in taking them?'

'Oh, yes please,' nodded Zoe.

There was also something else I wanted to mention to her, as I was determined to get Zoe a bed of her own and I'd been asking around.

'I spoke to Louisa the other day and Charlie's friend is getting rid of a double bed that he no longer needs,' I told her. 'I haven't got the room for it but I wondered if you might like it?'

'That would be brilliant,' replied Zoe.

'Charlie could even bring it round to your new place in his work van once you get the keys?'

'Thank you so, so much,' she smiled.

'Right,' I said, taking a final swig of tea. 'It's time for me to get going and leave you three to unpack.'

I went and found the girls and gave them a big hug.

'Now, this isn't really a proper goodbye,' I told them, 'because Mummy's going to bring you to my house soon and we can all have tea.'

'Can we play toys?' asked Lola.

'Yes,' I told her.

'And can we see Louisa and baby Edie?' asked Coco.

'I can certainly see if they'd like to come over too,' I replied.

The girls nodded and ran off to play.

'I don't think they're upset to see me go,' I joked to Zoe.

However, I could see that Zoe looked upset.

'I just want to say thank you for everything, Maggie,' she said quietly. 'You've been there for the girls and for me at the worst time in my life and I'll never ever be able to thank you enough. And I'll be forever grateful to you for talking me down that day.'

She swallowed a lump in her throat.

'I don't know what would have happened if you hadn't answered the phone to me.'

'It was my pleasure,' I told her. 'You're a brilliant mum. We all saw that and I hope you believe it now too.'

Zoe shrugged.

'I'm trying my best,' she said.

'Now go and be with those gorgeous girls of yours,' I smiled, giving her a farewell hug.

As I drove home, I just felt the creeping sadness that I always did when a child left my home. Everything felt very quiet, flat and strange somehow.

I sat on the sofa and took a rare moment to myself to enjoy the peace and quiet. This placement had felt like a whirlwind. Coco and Lola had only been with me for a few months but it felt as if so much had happened. After so much uncertainty, I was so pleased they were now reunited with their mother and looking forward to moving into their new house.

It was always a satisfying feeling when children were reunited with their birth parents. At the end of the day, Zoe was a loving, competent parent. I couldn't help but think that it had been society that had let her down, but this time she had help and support there if she needed it.

I willed myself to find the energy to get up off of the sofa At the end of a placement, I always felt drained and physically flat as my adrenalin levels dropped and I truly relaxed for the first time in months. I was about to get up and start making some tea for me and Amena, when my mobile rang.

It was Vicky.

Hi, lovey,' I said. 'The girls have just left.'

'That's great,' she told me. 'I hope you're doing OK.'

For once, she sounded really upbeat and cheerful.

'Guess what Maggie?' she told me. 'I've had a letter from the police. They're not going to press charges against me for assaulting Robert.'

'That's brilliant news,' I replied. 'I'm so glad they've seen sense.'

She read out the letter to me. 'We are very pleased to be able to confirm that having considered various forms of enquiry in the matter, we have decided that no further action will be taken against you. This means that no court proceedings will be instigated and that the police investigation has now concluded.'

'That must be such a relief for you,' I said.

'It really is,' she sighed. 'However, now the police investigation has ended, that means Social Services will start their enquiries.'

Having both attended training sessions about it, we knew

the process that had to be followed. Now Vicky's supervising social worker and her manager from her fostering agency would come round and talk to Vicky about the allegations the boys had made. Then they'd compile a report that they'd discuss at the next LADO (Local Authority Designated Officer) meeting where they'd decide whether the allegations were substantiated or not.

'The waiting is killing me,' Vicky confessed.

'It will all be fine,' I soothed. 'It's a really good sign that the police are not going to pursue any charges.

'I'm sure Social Services will do the same.'

'I hope so,' she replied.

All she could do now was stay positive and hopefully the boys would be back with her very soon.

'It's been a horrific few months but the nightmare is over now and it's all going to be OK,' I told her and I really meant it.

Acknowledgements

Thank you to my children, Tess, Pete and Sam, who are such a big part of my fostering today, although I had not met you when Amena, Coco and Lola came into my home. To my wide circle of fostering friends – you know who you are! Your support and your laughter are valued. To my friend Andrew B for your continued encouragement and care. Thanks also to Heather Bishop who spent many hours listening and enabled this story to be told, my literary agent Rowan Lawton and to Anna Valentine, Vicky Eribo and Beth Eynon at Seven Dials for giving me the opportunity to share these stories.

Maggie Hartley has fostered more than 300 children while being a foster carer for over twenty years. Taking on the children other carers often can't cope with, Maggie helps children that are deemed 'unadoptable' because of their behaviour or the extreme trauma that they've been through.

She's looked after refugees, supported children through sexual abuse and violence court cases, cared for teenagers on remand and taught young mums how to parent their new-born babies.

You can find her on Facebook at MaggieHartleyAuthor, where she would love to hear from you.

'I'm very, very bad. I don't deserve to have nice things. Nobody loves me.'

Three young siblings arrive at Maggie's door after being taken into care. Teachers of eight-year-old Bobby spotted distinct hand-shaped bruises on his arm and his dad and stepmother are uncooperative and hostile to Social Services. While they investigate, Bobby, as well as Melodie and Poppy, are looked after in Maggie's home.

As the children settle in, a thought won't let Maggie go. While Melodie and Poppy are clean, well-fed and immaculately dressed, Bobby is pale, severely underweight and extremely quiet. What looks like a case of neglect is actually something much more sinister. Bobby and his half-sisters are hiding a cruel secret, but can Maggie find the truth?

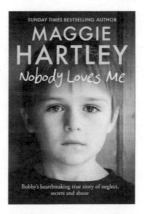

Read on for an extract from *Nobody Loves Me*, available now in paperback, eBook and audio

Stood on the doorstep was a woman in her thirties with dark curly hair wearing bright red lipstick. She was fashionably dressed with wide jeans, a striped jumper and a smart navy blue coat.

'Patsy?' I asked.

She looked so familiar but I couldn't place her.

'We've met before, haven't we?' I said and she nodded.

'Oh yes,' she said. 'I thought I recognised your name. You looked after Missy while we tried to find her a new placement.'

'Aah that's right,' I smiled. 'Sorry, my memory is terrible sometimes.'

'Oh don't worry, it was quite a few years ago now,' Patsy replied.

Missy had been a ten-year-old girl with autism and a lot of behavioural issues. She'd accused her foster carers of hitting her and, while the allegations were being investigated, she'd been immediately removed. She'd come to live with me in what was known as a bridging placement. In the end, things had broken down so badly with her former foster parents that she was moved to another carer. But it had taken nearly two months to find someone suitable who would take her on.

I couldn't keep her long-term as I already had Louisa with me permanently and I knew Missy needed one-to-one attention.

Back then, Patsy was a newly qualified social worker but she was good at her job and we'd got along well.

'How's Missy doing?' I asked her. 'Are you still her social worker?'

'Yes, I am,' smiled Patsy. 'She still has her challenges but she's moved to a specialist residential school now where she really seems to have settled.'

'I'm glad to hear it,' I nodded.

Although I would have loved to chat more, my mind suddenly focused back on the situation we were dealing with now. The one thing I'd noticed was that Patsy was standing on the doorstep alone.

'Where are the children?' I asked her, puzzled.

'Oh they're in the car,' she told me, gesturing to a red Nissan parked outside my house.

'I wanted to keep them out of the cold and have a quick word with you before I brought them in.'

'How are they doing?' I asked her.

'Tired, fed up and, as you'd imagine, very bewildered,' she shrugged.

I knew we couldn't leave them in the car for long so Patsy quickly ran through the basics. As Becky had said, it was a sibling group of three: Melodie was eleven, Poppy, ten, and there was eight-year-old Bobby.

'The school rang us this morning about suspicions of neglect,' she explained. 'The parents are hostile and clearly aren't willing to cooperate with us at this point so we had no choice but to go for an EPO.'

If Social Services believe that a child is in immediate danger, they can apply to the courts for an Emergency Protection Order, known as an EPO. A judge is always on call to deal with these and they can rush them through in a matter of hours.

I had so many questions but before Patsy could tell me any more, we heard someone knocking. In the glow of the street light, I could just make out a girl's face peering out of the back window of the car. She was tapping impatiently on the glass.

'I'd better go and bring them in as they'll be getting cold,' Patsy said, quickly heading off down the path.

I couldn't make out much in the gloom outside but I saw Patsy getting two purple rucksacks and a carrier bag out of the boot. Then a boy headed towards me up the path. He was small and looked much younger than eight.

'Hi, you must be Bobby,' I said gently. 'I'm Maggie.'

As I spoke, he looked up at me.

His blue eyes were big, blank and expressionless, and there were dark shadows underneath them. He had a thin face and his skin was so pale, it was almost translucent.

'Come on in and get warm,' I told him.

He wasn't wearing a coat and I could see that he was shivering.

His school uniform was an odd mishmash. His dirty trousers hung off him and were so long, they were trailing on the floor and had big holes in both knees. His blue school jumper was so small the sleeves finished at his elbows and it only went as far as his upper waist so it looked like a crop top. His shoes were tatty and worn and had split at the toes.

'Maggie, this is Bobby,' said Patsy, bustling up the path behind him.

'We've already met,' I smiled.

He stood in the hallway, not saying a word, staring down at the floor.

'And this is Melodie and Poppy,' said Patsy as she ushered the two girls forwards into the light of the hallway.

I was so surprised, I almost did a double take. I'd expected them to be pale, scruffy and thin just like their brother. But they were tall and heavyset with full faces and pink cheeks. Their eyes were bright and their long brown hair looked clean and glossy. They were both wearing matching pink puffer jackets and shiny black patent shoes.

'I'm Maggie,' I smiled. 'Come on in.'

'Do we have to?' scowled the taller girl who I assumed was the oldest, Melodie.

'I've explained this to you, Melodie,' Patsy told her patiently. 'Let's get you inside out of the cold and I'll go through it with you again.'

Her sister, Poppy, looked equally unimpressed.

'Let me take your coats,' I told the girls and they handed me their pink puffas.

'Did you bring a coat, Bobby?' I asked him but he looked down at the floor.

'I don't think Bobby had one with him or if he did, we've accidentally left it at school,' said Patsy.

'Not to worry,' I smiled. 'I've got plenty of warm coats in my cupboards.'

I led them into the living room at the front of the house. The girls flopped down on the sofa but Bobby stood there, his eyes still lowered to the floor.

'You can sit down too, flower,' I told him gently, leading him over to a chair.

There was a frailty about him – almost like if you touched him, he might break.

'I know you must all be hungry but I need to have a quick chat with Patsy,' I told them. 'So I'll get you a juice and a biscuit now and then I'll get you some dinner later.'

'I don't want nothing to eat,' scowled Poppy. 'I want to go home to Mummy.'

'I'm afraid that's not possible at the moment,' Patsy explained. 'Remember that we said you're going to stay the night at Maggie's house. We'll know more tomorrow when we talk to your parents.'

'I hate talking,' sighed Melodie. 'I just want to go back to our flat.'

'I can completely understand that,' I smiled sympathetically. 'And Patsy will let us know what's going on as soon as she can, but tonight you're going to stay here with me.'

The girls sat back begrudgingly. Patsy put the TV on and got them settled while I quickly got them a glass of juice and a biscuit from the kitchen.

When I came back in, *You've Been Framed* was on and they all seem transfixed.

'Maggie and I are just going to have a quick chat in the kitchen,' Patsy told them.

'We're only next door so shout out to us if you need anything,' I added.

None of them said a word as their eyes stayed glued to the screen.

Back in the kitchen, I put the kettle on and made Patsy and myself a cup of tea.

'Have the children eaten anything?' I asked her.

'Not really, just some snacky stuff at school,' she said.

'I've got a pasta bake keeping warm in the oven so I'll give that to them when you've gone,' I told her.

When the tea had brewed, I took it over to Patsy and sat down at the table with her.

'Thanks so much,' she sighed. 'It's been a long old afternoon.'

'So tell me what you know,' I said.

Patsy explained that teachers at the school had been concerned about Bobby for a while.

'Apparently he's extremely quiet and withdrawn and often wets himself. As you probably noticed yourself, Maggie, he's incredibly thin and his clothes are very tatty and dirty.'

She explained that teachers had called home a number of times to try to speak to his parents but no one ever got back to them and they had never turned up for his parents' evenings.

'What about the two girls?' I asked. 'Have their teachers noticed anything?'

'Well, that's the weird thing,' said Patsy. 'They don't have any obvious concerns about the girls, either about their appearance or behaviour. They're always clean and well turned out. They're engaged in class and I think Mum has been to school to see their teachers.'

She took a gulp of tea.

'But as you and I know, Maggie, girls are often better at hiding things so who knows what's really going on at home behind closed doors.'

She explained that the family wasn't previously known to Social Services and they'd had no involvement with the children before today.

'So why did the school call you?' I asked.

Patsy explained that when Bobby had been doing PE this morning, his class teacher had noticed bruises at the tops of both of his arms.

'They looked like fingertip bruises,' she told me. 'Like he'd been grabbed. There were also a couple of older, more faded bruises on his back.'

'Did they ask him how he'd got them?'

'Yes, but he didn't say very much or offer any reasonable explanation,' she replied. 'I think that combined with all of the concerns they'd been having about him anyway led his teacher to speak to the safeguarding person at school and she called Social Services.'

Patsy had gone up to the school and spoken to the teachers and then to Bobby.

'I asked him about the bruises and how he'd got them but, as I say, he didn't really say anything,' she told me. 'Then I spoke to the girls to ask them if they knew what had happened. They just told me that Bobby was silly and got into trouble all the time.'

The school had obtained one contact number for Mum, and Patsy had tried that but couldn't get through. So her manager had sent another social worker round to the flat.

'Mum answered, but she refused to engage or let the social worker in. There was lots of swearing, lots of claims that Bobby was a liar and that no one had done anything to him.

'There is a dad around apparently but there was no sign of him.'

The social worker had made it clear to the mother that none of the children would be returning home until they'd found out more.

'She explained that it was significant bruising, along with the concerns from school, which meant they needed to look into it more.'

'What did Mum say?' I asked.

'Nothing,' Patsy replied. 'She just slammed the door in my colleague's face.'

They'd spoken to their manager but they felt there was no other option at this stage than to go for an EPO.

'We've also got to involve the police now, so they'll probably go round tomorrow and see if that forces Mum to engage with us.'

Social Services' main priority is always to keep children safe, so even if there is the smallest element of doubt, they always prefer to err on the side of caution.

'Have they been examined by a medical professional?' I asked Patsy.

'Bobby has,' she replied. 'There's no indication the girls have been harmed so we didn't want to put them through an examination at this stage.'

Patsy had taken Bobby to see a GP. Social Services have a number of GPs in each area who work for them and are based at different medical centres.

The doctor examined Bobby and took photographs of his bruising.

He was underweight and small for his age, but thankfully there were no other obvious injuries except for the bruises. The GP had agreed the bruises looked like grab marks and were more than likely made by adult-sized fingers rather than something that would have happened if Bobby was playing with other children.

'The main aim this afternoon was to get them to a safe place for the night then we'll start looking into things again in the morning,' Patsy told me.

'No problem,' I said. 'And what are your thoughts about school tomorrow?'

'I think it's best they don't go in as we'll need to speak to the parents again and the police might want to talk to the children.'

That was a relief for me to hear. I knew the three of them would probably be exhausted after everything that had happened today and the idea of getting them all up and out the door to a school I'd never been to before would have felt like a real mission.

'Obviously they haven't come with any belongings or clothes except their school stuff,' Patsy told me.

'That's OK,' I smiled. 'I've got enough stuff in my cupboards so that we can make do tonight.'

It was getting late and I wanted to try to get the children fed and as settled as possible for the night. When we went back into the living room, they were still glued to the TV.

'I'm going to go now,' Patsy told them. 'But Maggie's going to look after you and I will see you tomorrow.'

They all looked shell-shocked and none of them said anything as I went to the front door to see Patsy out.

'I hope they're OK tonight,' she told me. 'I know the girls in particular are not happy but it's a situation that needs to be explored.'

'I'm sure they'll be fine,' I told her. 'Let's see what tomorrow brings.'

In these kinds of cases, no one knew what was going to happen. Sometimes when parents had calmed down, they were able to give an adequate explanation and the children were allowed to go home. A lot of the time in fostering, you were dealing with the unknown.

As I waved Patsy off, I felt slightly apprehensive about what the night ahead was going to bring. I had three worried, tired, and traumatised children sitting in my house and I was a complete stranger to them. All I could do was try my hardest to reassure them and make them feel as comfortable and settled as possible.

That was often the nature of being a foster carer. You had to be patient as you rarely got answers straight away.

I had to focus on the here and now. And that was getting them fed, washed and into bed. Then we would have to wait and see what tomorrow would bring.